General Introduction to Northeastern Literature in Exile

Bai Changqing

Translated by Lai Yonglong & Wang Chenyu

General Introduction to Northeastern Literature in Exile
Author: Bai Changqing
Translator: Lai Yonglong & Wang Chenyu
Language: English
Word Count (for space of all pages): 195 thousand words
Publisher: Chicago Academic Press
Number of Pages: 242
ISBN: 978-1-965890-72-1

Publishing	Chicago Academic Press
	5923 N Artesian Ave
	Chicago IL 60659
Email	contact@chicagoacademicpress.com
Website	http://chicagoacademicpree.com/
Book Size	6X9 inches
First Edution	October, 2025

Translator's Profile

The translator, Lai Yonglong, a current postgraduate student majoring in English Translation at the Graduate School of Translation and Interpreting, Jilin International Studies University, holds CATTI Level 3 and TEM-8 certifications, and has published academic papers in the field of translation studies.

The translator, Wang Chenyu, a current postgraduate student majoring in English Translation at the Graduate School of Translation and Interpreting, Jilin International Studies University, has won several national awards, holds the TEM-8 certificate, and has currently translated over 500,000 words.

Preface

This book is dedicated to "Northeastern Writers in Exile."

Half a century ago, in the northeastern region of the motherland, a young cohort of writers emerged. To this day, their names have endured in public memory, and their works continue to be widely celebrated as literary touchstones of their era. This formidable force, often referred to as the "The Northeast Literary Vanguard," made a bold and powerful entrance into the literary world, leaving a profound impact on its time and later becoming known as the "Northeastern Writers in Exile."

Understanding the masterworks and core writers among "Northeastern Writers in Exile" to grasp their literary importance, aesthetic value, and unique creativity within the wider scope of Chinese literary history is an endeavor of significant scholarly and cultural relevance.

Let us turn our gaze back to that profoundly tragic chapter in modern Chinese history.

The Mukden Incident of 1931, which occurred in Shenyang, shocked every Chinese person. At that time, what lay before everyone was the question of where the Chinese nation would go in the face of Japanese imperialist aggressors, and where each individual should go. Witnessing the magnificent land shuddering in the torment of blood and fire, how many Chinese people had their passionate blood stirred to a boiling point. At that pivotal moment in history, a group of writers, emerging from the northern regions, arrived, carrying with them the biting cold winds and snow of the North. They brought the anguished grief and seething resentment of the thirty million Northeast compatriots, who had endured the suffering of a fallen nation, and commenced penning defiant narratives of resistance. This collective embodied a literary advance unprecedented in China's historical narrative, a striking, vanguard power that embodied the spirit of the times. Their writings, steeped in sorrow and sacrifice, voiced the first cry of China's anti-war literary movement, heralding the dawn of a new era of nationwide anti-Japanese literature, and contributing profoundly to the historical record.

Over the course of the subsequent fourteen years, the Northeast was transformed into a grotesque and oppressive colony of Japanese imperialism, becoming the earliest and most profoundly devastated region in the country to endure the calamity of national disaster. This tragic fate sparked a vigorous spirit of national resurgence and defiance that, emerging from this land, not only preceded the rest of the nation but also came to define the prevailing aesthetic and ideological currents of the era. These writers emerged amidst a unique tapestry of historical and cultural circumstances that distinctly characterized their epoch, emerging at a time shaped by a combination of external and internal forces, which together formed the complex and defining coordinates of their era. The distinctive historical environment and the progression of events during that period inevitably shape a unique cultural context, which in turn gives birth to literary phenomena that align with and reflect the particularities of that time. Consequently, following the "The Mukden Incident," the withered region of Northeast saw the blossoming of anti-Japanese literature and the rise of the "Northeastern Writers in Exile" was an inevitable result of this complex interplay of historical and cultural forces.

A millennium's march has marched on, decades evaporating before our eyes, the literary trajectories once forged by those writers, some of which have faded into obscurity as time has blurred their paths, while others remain distinctly etched in the fabric of history and stand resolutely, awaiting future generations to uncover, understand, and critically assess them. The temporal distance of history allows us to approach this project in a more objective and static manner. Yet, it inevitably breeds unfamiliarity with the historical and cultural backdrop of that era, and the absence of firsthand experience remains an inescapable limitation. Consequently, this proves to be an arduous undertaking.

Whenever I recall those writers who, in their prime, commanded the literary world and devoted an immense body of brilliant works to the cultural heritage of our motherland, an image of towering, resilient poplar trees, deeply rooted in the vast expanse of the northern landscape, inevitably emerges in my mind, evoking within me a profound and wordless sense of reverence. In that moment, I am filled with a compelling sense of duty to honor and extol their legacy. They endured a life marked by relentless hardships and setbacks, yet their unyielding ambitions never faltered. Their upright and noble conduct, along with their monumental and expansive literary works, continue to evoke profound admiration and respect. In their time, they penned exceptional works such as *Village in August*, *The Field of Life and Death*, *Tales of Hulan River*, *Horqin Banner Grassland*, *Wanbao Mountain*, *On the Frontier*, *Children Without a Homeland*, *Sparks in the Cold Night*, and *The Seventh Pit*, each of which brought a fresh, combative spirit to the literary world at that time. Now, though that historical chapter lies far behind us, the spirit of that era, the invaluable spiritual wealth that the people still need, is something we must continue to preserve, is it not?

Long celebrated for their literary merit, the works of the "Northeastern Writers in Exile" have transcended regional boundaries, radiating influence across vast distances and even resonating with global audiences. Captivating generations of readers and earning admiration from people of various races and nations, they have come to be regarded not only as a cultural treasure for China but also for the entire world. Clearly, the creations of the "Northeastern Writers in Exile" possess not only artistic allure but also profound spiritual wealth, enabling people to gain an understanding of Northeast Chinese literature, modern Chinese literature, and, ultimately, the national spirit that defines the Chinese people.

Every time the dark night falls, I often find myself gazing up at the northern sky, where a cluster of stars, glowing with brilliance, draws my attention. Among the countless stars that sparkle in the vast expanse of the heavens, the Big Dipper, though not the most striking, remains a constant presence, its stars revolving steadfastly around the North Star, tracing endless circles in an eternal, unbroken motion. This unyielding journey, I believe, symbolizes the spirit of perseverance, the unwavering pursuit of a goal that never falters. High in the northern sky, it offers a sense of warmth to those who look up, and in my heart, it has come to represent the star of "Northeastern Writers in Exile." a symbol that will forever twinkle in the northern heavens, eternally etched in the memories of those who behold it.

On the occasion of the publication of this book, I would like to express my heartfelt gratitude to the colleagues at Chunfeng Literary and Art Publishing House, whose enthusiastic care and unwavering support have played a crucial role in bringing this work to fruition. In today's world, where publishing has become increasingly challenging, especially for serious academic works, their extraordinary perseverance deserves profound admiration, as they have continued striving despite numerous difficulties, even risking financial losses to ensure this book's release, a selfless commitment I will forever cherish and never forget.

Contents

Chapter 1 They Were Born on This Land

I. Not Just by Fate, But by Human Effort

Literature is the child of its time.

Any literary phenomenon, which never emerges without reason, is always in alignment with a particular socio-economic foundation and rooted in a specific socio-historical context.

In the 1930s, a group of young writers emerged in the northeastern region of the motherland, who would later be known as the "Northeastern Writers in Exile." Their emergence was not only a natural result of the social and historical developments in Northeast China at that time, but also a product of their ability to adapt to the specific environment, which included the region's unique geography, society, history, politics, economy, military circumstances, and intellectual and cultural landscape. Against this backdrop, the northeastern writers crafted a series of rich, dramatic, and imposing historical narratives, thereby leaving a dazzling and enduring cultural and historical legacy for future generations.

The ever-evolving social landscape, the tumultuous trials and tribulations of the people's fate, and the relentless struggle for the survival and future of the nation... In an era of unprecedented adversity in the history of Northeast China, history imbued literature with rich and profound significance, which indeed is an era that remains unforgettable, a distinctive and vast backdrop!

This backdrop was first and foremost shaped by the May Fourth Movement.

Reflecting on the early surge of the May Fourth Movement, a group of intellectuals, led by Chen Duxiu, were among the first to proclaim the slogans of "Democracy" and "Science," shaking the very foundations of feudal culture while simultaneously laying the groundwork for the emergence of new literature. Within this pioneering and foundational cultural movement, there already simmered a profound political passion aimed at saving the nation and restoring the dignity of the people, which served as the prelude to the advent of new literature in Northeast China.

During that period, new poetry and novels written in baihua ((vernacular Chinese, a form of written Chinese based on spoken language that became the main literary language during the May Fourth Movement), along with a wave of emerging literary figures and new literary groups, spread across the country in great numbers, much like mushrooms after a rain. Northeast region was also part of this movement, where new literature first took root in Fengtian (now Shenyang) and gradually spread northward from the south. Among the most prominent literary societies were the Baiyang Society, the Qiming Society, the Dongguang Society, the Chunchao Society, the Beilei Society, the Hanguang Drama Society, and the Canxing Society. The entire 1920s saw Northeast region's new literature flourishing, marking a time when the realist literary spirit of the May Fourth Movement became deeply rooted and gradually evolved in the region.

At that time, several newspapers in Northeast region also became enthusiastic promoters of the new literature. In the late 1920s, the *Xinmin Evening News*, *Pingmin Daily* and *the Shengjing Times* from Fengtian, and *the Taidong Daily* from Dalian were all actively supportive of new literary works, reprinting the latest works of prominent authors such as Lu Xun, Ye Shengtao, Guo Moruo, Wen Yiduo, Hu Shi, Wang Tongzhao, and Xu Zhimo, whose efforts played a significant role in fostering the growth of literary newcomers and promoting the spread of new literature in Northeast China.

Mao Dun, in his evaluation of the literary activities during this period, remarked: "The movement was primarily driven by young students and intellectuals from various professional fields. Although their organizations and publications might have appeared and disappeared in quick succession, their impact on the development of new literature was undeniable. The seemingly chaotic and somewhat wasted group activities, along with the publication of small-scale journals in these years, can be liked to the great flood of the Nile River, which was soon followed by a surge of hopeful young writers." (*The Catena of Chinese New Literature: Volume I of Novels [Introduction]*).

This prophecy is destined to come true.

In Northeast region, the first group of young writers, as anticipated, indeed made their appearance. Among them were notable figures such as Wang Zhuoran, Zhu Huanjie, Luo Muhua, and Wang Lianyou. Most of these writers lived within the social circles of the petite bourgeoisie, and their literature remained in its early stages. The themes of their works frequently revolved around the pursuit of individual freedom and marital autonomy, while also challenging traditional feudal morals, where this shared characteristic was a hallmark of the literature emerging from the first stage of the May Fourth Movement's ideological liberation. In this regard, Lu Xun offered an insightful analysis, stating: "In contemporary Chinese society, the most likely works to emerge are those that express the rebellious spirit of the petite bourgeoisie, either in resistance or in exposure." (Lu Xun, *Two Hearts Collection: A Glimpse of Shanghai Literature*).

From the late 1920s to the early 1930s, a significant turning point in Northeast China's history unfolded, and the same can be said for its literature. During this period, the distinctive "Northeastern" characteristics gradually became more apparent, and its individuality began to stand out in contrast to the literature of the interior regions of China. Rather than merely following the developmental pace of literature in the south of the Great Wall, Northeast literature carved out and established its own unique position, marked by its distinctive traits and distinct identity. After The Mukden Incident in 1931, it embarked on a completely new and unique path, with its revolutionary and anti-war consciousness at the core, leading the way in Chinese literature, which marked the overall pattern of the evolving relationship between the development of new literature in Northeast region and that of the regions in the south of the Great Wall at the time.

The core spirit of the May Fourth New Literature is clearly defined by its close connection to the social realities of China. While it aimed at transforming the old culture, it also possessed a distinct critical and innovative nature. From the very outset, political elements were subtly embedded within it, and once it encountered the specific historical context of Northeast China, it swiftly adopted the theme of resisting Japanese aggression and saving the nation, thereby merging the new literature with the political goals of patriotism and anti-imperialism, which became the defining feature of the development of new literature in Northeast China. A group of young literary figures from the Northeast region, who emerged from the wave of New Literature, demonstrated a particularly acute ability to capture patriotic ideologies and a historically charged eagerness to articulate them. Among them, the budding of "Northeastern Writers in Exile" began to take shape.

The reason why the higher levels of Northeast New Literature were able to foster the "Northeastern Writers in Exile" lies in the unique historical and social environment that characterized Northeast society from the late 1920s to the early 1930s.

At the turn of the 20th century, the geographical and historical landscape of Northeast region grew peculiarly precarious. Strategically positioned at the intersection of Russian and Japanese imperialist spheres of influence, it was squeezed between the clashing interests of these two powers, painstakingly struggling to maintain its autonomy. Since the 19th century, Russia had been advancing southward by crossing the Heilongjiang River, while Japan pushed westward by encroaching on Korea. These actions turned Northeast China into a periphery for their imperialist expansion, a territory they coveted. By the late 1920s, Japanese imperialism had rapidly escalated its influence in the region, fueling recurring diplomatic clashes with China. Japan's aggressive ambitions now posed a direct threat to Northeast China's security, a palpable danger that even ordinary locals perceived. Within the Northeast region, the Fengtian warlords clung to their bellicose policies, which not only plunged the region into perpetual conflict but also accelerated the collapse of its agrarian feudal economy. The entire Northeast resembled a decaying edifice, battered by relentless storms, its instability intensifying by the day. All the while, the shadow of a historic upheaval began to creep over the land.

In the late 1920s, proletarian literature (known as "Pro Literature" in Chinese leftist discourse) not only rapidly gained momentum in Northeast China but also became a catalyst for the "Northeastern Writers in Exile" to take shape.

In 1929, under the direction of the Chinese Communist Party's Manchurian Provincial Committee, a group of young students in Fengtian founded *Ice Flower (Binghua)*, a progressive literary journal. Meanwhile, CCP underground operatives consolidated editorial control over *Guanwai (Beyond the Pass)*, another proletarian publication. On the campus of Northeast University, figures like Bai Xiaoguang (pen name Ma Jia), Lin Jirong, Zhang Luwei, Li Yingshi, Ye Youquan, and Shen Changyan began publishing essays in local periodicals, emerging as rising voices of dissent. Following *Guanwai*'s example, these young intellectuals launched the left-leaning *Beiguo (Northern Realm)*, followed shortly by *Nuchao (Tide of Fury)*. Works published in *Beiguo* and *Nuchao* including Li Yingshi's treatise *Literature and Class*, Bai Xiaoguang's novel *Mother*, and his epic poem *In the Mountains and Ridges*, pulsed with revolutionary fervor, marking a radical shift in Northeast China's cultural landscape.

In Northern Manchuria, Luo Feng, a CCP underground operative, launched the first proletarian journal, *Zhi Xing Monthly (Knowledge and Action)*, among railway workers in early 1930. Meanwhile, fellow Party member Jin Jianxiao oversaw the literary supplements of *Chenguang Bao (Dawn Gazette)* and *Dabei Xinbao (Great Northern News)* in Harbin. During this period, leftist intellectuals aligned with the CCP also gained control over cultural sections such as the *Wenyi (Literature)* supplement of Harbin's *Guoji Xiebao (International Cooperation Daily)* and Changchun's *Datong Daily's Ye*

Shao (Night Sentinel). Writers including Jiang Chunfang, Luo Feng, Shu Qun, Bai Lang, Xiao Jun, Xiao Hong, Jin Jianxiao, Kong Luosun, Jin Ren and Saike contributed prolifically to these platforms. They gathered clandestinely in teahouses and rented apartments, forming underground theater troupes and organizing subversive art exhibitions critiquing social inequality that galvanized Harbin's radical cultural scene in the early 1930s. The "Harbin Writers' Group" became the precursor to what would later emerge as the "Northeastern Writers in Exile."

At that time, the dissemination of progressive foreign literature in Northeast China played a significant role in the emergence of the "Northeastern Writers in Exile." Many writers grew under the intellectual influence of revolutionary literature from abroad. In progressive bookstores in Fengtian and Dalian, works by Japanese progressive writers such as Takiji Kobayashi and Tokunaga Sunao were available, among which *The Crab Cannery Ship* had a particularly profound impact, having been read by many young progressive literary enthusiasts. Meanwhile, in Northern Manchuria, Soviet revolutionary literature exerted an even greater influence. Newspapers such as *International Cooperation Daily* and *Greater North New Daily* introduced the works and biographies of Maxim Gorky and Vladimir Mayakovsky, publishing Soviet literary pieces that significantly shaped the literary aspirations of the time's young writers.

In the early 1930s, within this particular historical period and across the unique geographical landscape of Northeast China, several distinct cultural forces, originating from different directions and belonging to various traditions, collided and merged with one another. At their point of convergence, a "T-shaped" cultural crossroads emerged, where the interaction and expansion of these influences gave birth to a new sub-literary sphere. The rise of progressive young writers who remained committed to the dominant current of realism ultimately provided the necessary human talent for the emergence of the "Northeastern Writers in Exile." The gunfire of the Mukden

Incident served as the final catalyst, uniting all the preexisting conditions. From that moment on, the "Northeastern Writers in Exile" surged forth like a flood released through an opened gate, unstoppable in their momentum.

II. Contingency and Inevitability

The Mukden Incident not only led to Northeast China becoming a Japanese colony, but also marked the beginning of China's War of Resistance, ushering in a new era in Chinese history.

During the Mukden Incident, most of the "Northeastern Writers in Exile" were still in their homeland, where they witnessed the process of the territory's fall. The young writers were deeply pierced by the military hymns of the Japanese invaders, their rising sun flag, and their arrogant occupation, as well as by the indiscriminate killings, abuses, and the agonizing cries and struggles of the Northeast people. The harsh reality forced them to speak out, and their patriotism made it impossible for them to accept the fate of becoming slaves to foreign invaders. As a result, they fled to the region south of the Great Wall, wandering far and wide. They personally endured the pain of losing both their homes and their country, suffering at the hands of the invaders. For them, personal misfortune and national disaster, individual fate and the fate of the entire nation, suddenly became inseparably intertwined in a way never before experienced. "Every social crisis and transformation inevitably heightens the unpredictability of individual fate, particularly increasing one's awareness of this unpredictability." (Quoted from Northeast writer Yu Heiding, in Shen Weiwei's paper *A Brief Discussion on the Rise of the Northeast Writer Group*). Confronted by such sudden historical upheavals, these young writers became more profoundly anxious about the fate of their country and nation. They did not take up writing in order to become writers, but to save their homeland, their people, and themselves. By this time, their creative mindset had undergone a profound transformation compared to the period before the "Mukden Incident." What began as shock and sorrow at the harsh reality soon gave way to indignation and resistance. Driven by a strong desire to express their emotions, they began to yearn for the battle to reclaim their homeland. This inner longing, perfectly in tune with the prevailing currents of the era, also mirrored the collective wishes of the people. Xiao Jun recalled, "My motivation and primary purpose in engaging in literary creation were very simple: it was for the true independence of our country, the complete liberation of our nation, and the genuine emancipation of the people, leading to the emergence of a society free from exploitation and oppression." (*A Brief Overview of My Literary Career*, Xiao Jun). His statement is both sincere and to the point. Li Huiying also stated in her autobiography, "It was after the Mukden Incident in 1931, when I was filled with anger at losing the cities of Shenyang and Changchun overnight, and just as quickly losing vast territories of Northeast China and three million people being enslaved, that I was moved to take up the pen and write." Ma Jia recalled, "In 1931, after the Mukden Incident, I fled to Beiping, losing my education, my livelihood, and all my basic rights to live... In the summer of 1932, driven by a desire to experience life firsthand, I resolutely returned to my homeland in Northeast China, where I spent two years in the countryside as an exiled youth. Under the oppressive political climate of the time, what I faced was the reign of terror brought by the enemy's brutal oppression and the heavy chains that shackled the farmers. The harsh reality was suffocating and infuriating, and with a deep sense of defiance, I bid farewell to the land that had been humiliated..." (*Afterword to Sparks in the Cold Night*, Ma Jia). The Mukden Incident not only caused a dramatic shift in the history and destiny of Northeast China but also marked a profound turning point in the lives of these young writers, whose peaceful homes were suddenly lost, forcing them into exile and perpetual displacement, all while witnessing the tragic fate of their fellow countrymen. The observations and experiences they encountered in their daily lives greatly broadened their horizons, and they seamlessly wove their creative work into the turbulent currents of social change. With a deep sense of social responsibility as writers, they awakened the national consciousness of impending disaster and poured their emotions into creating works centered on the themes of resisting Japanese aggression and saving the nation. Through this transformation, their inner feelings were also sublimated, giving rise to a new artistic identity and vision.

The "Northeastern Writers in Exile" were deeply immersed in a historical and cultural collision of unprecedented scale, an experience that not only liberated them from the suffocating constraints of traditional ideologies but also empowered them to attain spiritual freedom, allowing their creative individuality to emerge and enabling them to express their beliefs without restraint. Born amidst the sudden tempests of a transformative era, weathered unforgettable emotional trials and countless hardships, a dual fate of personal misfortune and unique privilege. It was precisely within this maelstrom of historical upheaval that they cultivated fresh perspectives to comprehend life and society. Their creative consciousness, undeniably more complex than that of writers untouched by life's crucible, bore the scars of internal conflicts and agonizing choices. Through their odyssey, they wandered in uncertainty, writhed in anguish, wrestled with confusion, and occasionally succumbed to the melancholy of disillusionment. Yet their conviction in both the triumph of the Anti-Japanese War and Northeast China's radiant future burned unquenchable. When history's crucible tested their mettle, they courageously chose adaptation over escapism, meeting epochal challenges head-on. Without such spiritual fortitude, the literary works of these "Northeastern Writers in Exile" would never have attained the profound historical resonance and soul-stirring power that continues to move generations.

In the south of the Great Wall, these writers ascended as luminous constellations, their individual brilliance converging into a radiant beacon that illuminated the literary firmament.

In 1932, Li Huiying, a writer from Jilin who had fled south of the Great Wall, made his literary debut by publishing his first short story, *The Last Lesson*, in *Beidou*, a left-wing journal under the editorship of Ding Ling, which marked a significant moment as it became the first work by a Northeast writer in exile to address the pressing issue of anti-Japanese resistance and the fight for the salvation of Northeast China. In May 1933, Li Huiying's novel *Wanbao Mountain* made its debut, drawing inspiration from the real-life Wanbao Mountain Incident, a conflict orchestrated by Japanese aggressors in Jilin Province on the eve of the Mukden Incident. Through its narrative, the novel vividly portrays the intensifying economic exploitation carried out by Japan and the resulting fierce resistance from the Chinese people. While its structural composition may appear somewhat loosely arranged and its literary techniques not entirely polished, its thematic innovation and historical relevance render it a groundbreaking work. As the first full-length novel by a Northeast writer in exile that explicitly centers on the anti-Japanese struggle, *Wanbao Mountain* holds significant literary and historical value. Together with Zhang Tianyi's *Gears* and Yang Hansheng's *The Volunteer Army*, it was included in the renowned "Anti-War Creative Series," published by Shanghai's Hufeng Publishing House, garnering widespread attention and marking an important moment in the evolution of wartime literature.

Between 1935 and 1936, as the husband-and-wife literary duo Xiao Jun and Xiao Hong who had come to Shanghai, were the first to publish their famous novels *Village in August* and *The Field of Life and Death*. Mr. Lu Xun wrote prefaces for these two novels, pointing out that "their descriptions of the tenacity for life and the struggle against death often penetrate the very paper" (*Introduction to The Field of Life and Death,* Lu Xun) and "this is exactly the heart of slaves!" And he stated, "Any reader with a conscience can finish reading it and will gain something from it." (*Introduction to Village in August,* Lu Xun) Mr. Lu Xun's praise and cultivation suddenly made the names of the Northeast writers resound, and the true value of their works began to be recognized by people. Shu Qun, who arrived in Shanghai later than Xiao Jun and Xiao Hong, wrote the famous short story *Child Without a Motherland*, which was highly praised. Luo Feng wrote the famous short story *The Seventh Pit*, depicting the scenes after Shenyang fell. Luo Binji wrote the novel *On the Frontier*, which showed the life of the early anti-Japanese guerrilla forces in Northeast China. Ma Jia wrote the novella *Before and After the Coronation* (also known as *Sparks in the Cold Night*), depicting the tragic real-life scenes of the rural areas in Northeast China before and after the puppet Manchukuo emperor's "coronation". Duanmu Hongliang wrote the long novel *Horqin Banner Grassland*, presenting the grand appearance of the rural areas in Northeast China on the eve of the Mukden Incident. The passionate and tragic recitation poems by Mu Mutian and Gao Lan who had fled to the areas south of the Great Wall, the plays by Yang Hui and Sai Ke, the short stories by Yu Heding and Lin Jue, and the translated works by Jin Ren were all successively published. A large group of young "Northeastern Writers in Exile" began to be active in the literary circles in the areas south of the Great Wall. Their works unfold against vast and sweeping landscapes, imbued with profound thematic significance. From the quiet northern town of Hulan to the rural villages along the Liao River in southern Manchuria, from the borderland scenery of Hunchun to the bustling streets of Northeast China's cities, from the snow-capped peaks of Changbai Mountain to the boundless expanse of the Khorchin grasslands—each setting becomes a canvas upon which the anguish, resilience, and unyielding spirit of the Northeast people are vividly inscribed. Through their words, the piercing cries of those who endured the horrors of the Mukden Incident echo, the silent tears of thirty million displaced compatriots flow, and the awakening consciousness and defiant resistance of a people rise like an unstoppable tide. In just a short span of two or three years, a remarkable wave of literary works emerged, collectively depicting the resistance struggles in Northeast China, while a sudden influx of displaced "Northeastern Writers in Exile" arrived in the literary circles of south of the

Great Wall. Like a powerful gust of wind surging through a mountain pass, their presence sent ripples across the literary landscape. Their works, focusing on life in the occupied Northeast, a subject of nationwide concern yet largely unfamiliar to the general populace, garnered immediate academic recognition. This phenomenon not only led to the identification of anti-Japanese salvation literature as a new literary domain, but also solidified the ideological value of these writings. Consequently, the "Northeastern Writers in Exile" gradually coalesced into a discernible literary collective during this period. Their creations brought to China's interior literary circles an unprecedented repertoire featuring "unexplored settings, innovative themes, original character archetypes, and novel historical contexts"[1], a transformative contribution whose profound impact far exceeded the writers' own expectations.

In the late 1930s, the literary creations of the "Northeastern Writers in Exile" continued to develop. Xiao Jun produced the long novel *The Past Years*, which depicted rural life in western Liaoning, as well as short story collections such as *Sheep* and *On the River*. Xiao Hong authored the renowned novel *Tales of Hulan River*, along with short stories including *March in a Small Town*, *Hands*, and *On the Ox Cart*. Together, Xiao Jun and Xiao Hong co-authored the short story collection *Trek*. Duanmu Hongliang published the short story collection *Hatred* and the novella *The Ocean of the Land*. Luo Binji released several works reflecting the resistance of people in Kuomintang-controlled areas and his own family history, including the short story collection *Spring in Beiwangyuan* and the novels *Childhood* and *The Family History of Jiang Buwei*. Luo Feng authored the short story collection *By the Hulan River* and novellas such as *Return* and *Mo Yun and Second Lieutenant Han Ermo*. Shu Qun published the lyrical long poem *In the Hometown*, the novellas *The Old Soldier* and *A Secret Story*, and short story collections like *Children Without a Homeland* and *Beyond the Sea*. Li Huiying wrote essay

[1] Qiao Mu: *Review of "Village in August"*, *The China Times*, February 25, 1936

collections such as *The Rebirth Collection*, *Between Soldiers and Civilians*, and *Wild Inns in the Valley*, which depicted wartime life in Kuomintang-controlled areas and expressed nostalgia for his homeland. Bai Lang wrote novellas including *The Rebel Son* and *The Chilling Halo*. Ma Jia produced the lyrical long poems *The Fire Sacrifice* and *March of the Ancient Capital*, as well as short stories such as *Family Letters* and *We Have Ancestors*. Sai Ke became a renowned lyricist, writing songs such as *Thirty Million Refugees*, *March of the Manchurian Prisoners*, and *The Song of the Northeast National Salvation Association*. Following his poetry collection *Traveling Heart*, Mu Mutian published two more poetry collections, *The Song of the Exiles* and *A New Journey*. Lin Jue authored short story collections including *The Mountain Village*, *Under the Lash*, and *Kindling*. In addition, the literary activities of Yu Heiding, Gao Lan, Kong Luosun, Jin Ren, Yang Shuo, Liu Shude, Shi Tianshou, Gao Tao, and Yelin were also highly active. Within just a few years, Northeast writers had emerged as a powerful new force within the left-wing literary movement in the south of the Great Wall.

III. The Hearts of the Slaves

After entering the south of the Great Wall, Northeast writers had more frequent interactions with left-wing writers, which broadened their perspectives, enriched their life experiences, and provided them with a relatively stable environment for writing. Notably, several key writers such as Xiao Jun, Xiao Hong, Luo Feng, Shu Qun, Bai Lang, Jin Ren, Lin Jue, and Li Huiying, unexpectedly yet simultaneously gravitated toward Shanghai around 1934, gathering within the Left League. This convergence was a choice of profound significance.

Shanghai was the epicenter of progressive cultural activities in China at the time, a battlefield where revolutionary literature fiercely clashed with reactionary literature. For the progressive writers from Northeast China, who longed to engage in the struggle, the city naturally held immense appeal. As their works on the theme of resisting Japanese aggression were about to be published, they arrived in Shanghai and immediately immersed themselves in the surging tide of revolutionary literature, undergoing the baptism of ideological struggle, an experience of great significance for their personal and artistic growth. At that time, it was the progressive cultural circles of Shanghai that were best equipped to truly understand and appreciate the innovative value of their works, and it was also only within the progressive cultural circles of Shanghai that their literary contributions could be widely disseminated and their status firmly established.

Shanghai's Association of Chinese Left-Wing Writers warmly embraced the broader progressive cultural circles, extending its support with the care of an elder, nurturing these young literary talents from the North like delicate seedlings and creating a favorable environment for them to showcase their abilities. Influential literary journals in Shanghai, such as *Literature*, *Writers*, and *Mainstream*, provided them with platforms to publish their works, giving them opportunities to gain recognition. Additionally, several renowned writers and critics enthusiastically promoted and reviewed their works, helping to amplify their voices within the literary scene.

Luo Binji's first full-length novel, *On the Frontier*, was directly recommended and facilitated for publication by Mao Dun. Similarly, Duanmu Hongliang's short story *The Melancholy of Cilu Lake* benefited from the encouragement and support of Mao Dun and Zheng Zhenduo. Works such as *Village in August*, *The Field of Life and Death*, *Children Without a Homeland*, *Horqin Banner Grassland*, and *The Melancholy of Cilu Lake* received immediate attention upon their release, garnering enthusiastic support and promotion from esteemed writers including Mao Dun, Ding Ling, Zhou Libo, Zhou Yang, Qiao Mu, and Hu Feng.

When commenting on Shu Qun's *Children Without a Homeland*, Zhou

Libo remarked: “His characters are simple, straightforward, and courageous, possessing an independent spirit and a proud temperament... They refuse to tolerate any oppression imposed upon themselves or their nation, which stands in stark contrast to the servile acceptance of foreign oppression exhibited by many of our compatriots. A China striving for liberation desperately needs such characters.”[1] In his review of *Village in August*, Qiao Mu said: “*Village in August*, along with its author, has arrived at the foreign concessions, and thus everyone is filled with admiration. ... There have been works written about Manchuria, and there have been works written about war, but never before has there been a piece that combines Manchuria and war in such a way. ...This book allows us to see the true picture of the revolutionary war in Manchuria. ...These are exactly the things that the Chinese people are eager to understand, and this book reports them with passionate writing.”[2] Hu Feng commented on *The Melancholy of Cilu Lake*, describing it as creating a “tragically beautiful and moving picture” of the suffering of its characters. “This is not a bloody story, yet readers can still feel the tragic lives of Chinese farmers on the Manchurian land.”[3] In addition, comments such as Wang Tongzhao praising *The Ocean of the Land* as “sturdy and vigorous,”[4]and Ba Ren praising *Horqin Banner Grassland* for “standing up the Horqin Banner Grassland” (as seen in *Northeast Modern Literature Materials*, Volume 5, Page 153), are both fair and insightful reviews. These critiques accurately highlight the distinctive value of the works of the “Northeastern Writers in Exile.”

The recognition of the status of Northeast progressive writers exiled to Shanghai is also closely linked to the direct support of Mr. Lu Xun, who warmly received Xiao Jun and Xiao Hong, and resolutely refuted the

---

[1] Zhou Libo: *A Retrospective on Novel Writing in 1936—A Year of Abundance, Guangming Journal*, No.2, Volume 2, 1937

[2] Qiao Mu: Review of “Village in August”, The China Times, February 25, 1936

[3] Hu Feng: *The Breath of the Living, Mainstream Journal*, Issue 3, Volume 1, 1936

[4] Wang Tongzhao: *Postscript by the Editor, Literature*, No.8, Volume 2

criticisms made by Dick (Zhang Chunqiao) regarding *Village in August*, which claimed that the novel had many issues both in technique and content, and mockingly suggested that "the Japanese army should not have returned from Northeast China so early".[1] Lu Xun's defense of these young Northeast writers protected them from such disparaging attacks. Mr. Lu Xun, despite his frail health, wrote prefaces for *Village in August* and *The Field of Life and Death*, and arranged for their publication under the "Slave Series." He viewed these works as literature for the slaves. Lu Xun believed that such sharp and impactful works were exactly what was needed in Shanghai and China at that time—works that would awaken the "numb" hearts of the slaves and straighten the spine of the nation.

Mr. Lu Xun said, "We must tell everyone about the suffering of those who are doomed to become slaves of foreign races...We must not let them reach the conclusion that it is better to remain slaves of our own kind rather than become slaves of others." (*Half-Summer Collection*, Lu Xun). This profound reflection and heartfelt hope about the national soul could only have been expressed by Lu Xun himself. At the end of his preface for *The Field of Life and Death*, Mr. Lu Xun left behind a deeply emotional and meaningful passage:

"Now, on the night of November 14, 1935, I am reading *The Field of Life and Death* again under the lamp. The surroundings are eerily silent, with the familiar voices of my neighbors no longer heard, the usual calls of street vendors absent, and only the occasional distant bark of a dog. It occurs to me that the British and French concessions were not like this, and neither was Harbin; there, my fellow residents and I lived in different worlds, each harboring different feelings. Yet now, my heart feels like water in an ancient well, without a ripple, numbly writing the words above. This is the heart of a slave! — But if it still disturbs the reader's heart, then we are definitely not

[1] Zhang Chunqiao: *We Must Implement Self-Criticism*, supplement *Torch* of *The Great Evening News*, March 15, 1936

slaves."

Mr. Lu Xun, through the countless bodies of slaves, loudly shouted, "We are definitely not slaves." The Northeast writers were also shouting, "We are not slaves." Mr. Lu Xun's heart resonated with theirs, and this shared sentiment is the heart of the slaves.

In 1930s Shanghai, the fate of progressive literature was fraught with peril, as the left-wing cultural movement struggled to survive and resist under the relentless repression of the White Terror. This period of political oppression created an atmosphere where even Mr. Lu Xun felt a profound sense of loneliness in his heart. Yet, it was precisely during this dark and turbulent time that *Village in August* and *The Field of Life and Death* emerged, much to Lu Xun's great delight, who saw with clarity the immense value these works held, recognizing that they were not only urgently needed but also perfectly timed for the moment. These works were of monumental significance, and like roosters heralding the first light of dawn, they marked the arrival of a new era in national resistance literature.

Chapter 2 Historical Reflection and Contemplation

I. The Rooster's Call Heralding the Dawn

The emergence of the "Northeastern Writers in Exile" marked the beginning of a significant literary mission, one that involved venturing into a new and uncharted literary realm, devoid of any pre-existing models to follow, forcing them to forge their own path, which was intrinsically tied to the inheritance and promotion of the spirit of the May Fourth Movement, and their works distinctly reflected the era's spirit, the national character, and revolutionary ideals, embodying a forward-looking momentum. These writers' creations were deeply attuned to the times, closely mirroring the social realities of Northeast China, with a primary mission of portraying the essence of "life," and emphasizing the historical significance of "resisting Japanese aggression and saving the nation." This theme encapsulated the central spirit of the "Northeastern Writers in Exile" works. Through their timely and profound engagement with the awakening spirit in response to national peril, they harmonized it with the harsh realities of life in Northeast China, thereby representing the core of the May Fourth realist literary tradition.

Before the Mukden Incident, although works with anti-imperialist themes existed, they had yet to form the mainstream of new literature. However, following the Mukden Incident, a significant shift occurred as national contradictions gradually ascended to become the primary domestic conflict. This shift also transformed the focus of new literature, with the theme of anti-Japanese resistance and national salvation—fundamentally representing the collective will of the people—emerging as the dominant force within the literary landscape of the time. The works of the "Northeastern Writers in Exile" effectively captured the latent concerns of the people regarding the fate of their nation, weaving these anxieties into the fabric of everyday life and revealing a unique aesthetic rooted in strength. Within the context of Northeast

Chinese society, where the anti-Japanese sentiment and actions of the people were deeply embedded, these writers found solid ground for expressing this aesthetic historical movement. In their narratives, the vast expanse of Northeast farmers, students, and ordinary working-class individuals took center stage, bearing the heavy burden of national liberation, and through their fearless struggles, they illuminated the path toward the future of the Chinese nation, thereby elevating the theme of anti-imperialist patriotism in new literature to a more profound and elevated level.

Literature's reflection of real life generally takes two distinct forms: one being a passive, closed reflection, and the other a more dynamic, progressive, and open reflection. The creative works of the "Northeastern Writers in Exile" belong to the latter category, representing a form of literature that intensifies and exposes the harsh realities of life, infusing with a critical and combative spirit.

Their works were the first to introduce to the entire nation the true nature of Northeast society under Japanese and puppet rule, vividly depicting the suffering endured by the people of Northeast China at the time, which provided an authentic portrayal of the specific historical and social conditions of the region, illustrating the intricate and complex class relationships. Moreover, they emphasized that the root cause of the suffering faced by the Northeast people was the invasion of Japanese imperialism.

Xiao Hong's novel *The Field of Life and Death* stands out in its depiction of the changes in Northeast rural life against this backdrop. Before the Mukden Incident, feudal forces ruthlessly exploited the labor of farmers. The impoverished rural woman, Wang Po, sells her only old horse, but only receives the price of its hide in return. Despite such extreme poverty, life could not continue in this way. When the sound of the Mukden Incident artillery was heard, the banners of "benevolent rule" arrived: "The village girls all ran away...a thirteen-year-old girl was taken away by the Japanese." "There were hardly any chickens left in the whole village," and "under the banner of 'benevolent rule,' more fields were left fallow." Wang Po, reflecting on the painful days of the past, longed to retrieve those days, for the present was even worse than yesterday. Under Japanese rule, the so-called "benevolent rule" led to the complete collapse of the Northeast rural economy, with farmers reduced to political slavery and subjected to intensified economic exploitation. Through the tragic experiences of ordinary farmers like Wang Po, Zhao San, Er Li Ban, and Jin Zhi, the novel illustrates the harsh reality they endured, revealing that no matter whether they went to the cities or sought refuge in Buddhist monasteries, they could not escape the cannibalistic world they were trapped in (as noted by Hu Feng in the *Postscript to The Field of Life and Death*).

Luo Feng's short story *The Seventh Pit* presents a harrowing and vivid portrayal of Northeast society, depicting the tragic and brutal incident in which Japanese soldiers mercilessly bury Chinese civilians alive in Shenyang. Through this chilling event, the story exposes the indescribable savagery and inhumanity of the Japanese invaders. Similarly, Lin Jue's novels *Mountain City* and *The Hoe*, along with works by other authors, authentically and sharply reveal the darkness of the Japanese and puppet rule, effectively shedding light on the horrific realities of occupation.

Ma Jia's "The Fire in the Cold Night" plunges even further into the harsh realities of the most impoverished rural communities. One particularly striking chapter meticulously details the heavy taxes and arbitrary levies forced upon the farmers to commemorate the puppet Manchukuo Emperor's "coronation." The village head, in the village office, announces a bewildering list of charges that includes "railway guard fees, county cavalry regiment fees, costs for receiving Japanese officials, security expenses, village office operational costs, hospitality fees, road repair expenses, political work miscellaneous costs, flood relief charges, spring plowing loans, university heating fees, and national flag production costs," among others. The sheer volume and diversity of this list are deeply shocking, serving as a clear and vivid chart that starkly reveals the class exploitation within Northeast rural society, exposing the tragic plight of the farmers during that period. This vast ruling coalition, consisting of the Japanese occupiers, the puppet government, and the landowners, colluded with one another, using the military might of the Japanese invaders as their support to control the destiny of the ordinary farmers. The resulting atmosphere of "unrelenting cold nights," where life and death are perilously close, and the people are struggling to survive on the brink of death, encapsulates the specific historical reality of Northeast society. This dire situation, where national contradictions had escalated into the central conflict, is powerfully conveyed and explained through the narrative.

Ma Jia's *Sparks in the Cold Night* plunges even further into the harsh realities of the most impoverished rural communities. One particularly striking chapter meticulously details the heavy taxes and arbitrary levies forced upon the farmers to commemorate the puppet Manchukuo Emperor's "coronation." The village head, in the village office, announces a bewildering list of charges that includes "railway guard fees, county cavalry regiment fees, costs for receiving Japanese officials, security expenses, village office operational costs, hospitality fees, road repair expenses, political work miscellaneous costs, flood relief charges, spring plowing loans, university heating fees, and national flag production costs," among others. The sheer volume and diversity of this list are deeply shocking, serving as a clear and vivid chart that starkly reveals the class exploitation within Northeast rural society, exposing the tragic plight of the farmers during that period. This vast ruling coalition, consisting of the Japanese occupiers, the puppet government, and the landowners, colluded with one another, using the military might of the Japanese invaders as their support to control the destiny of the ordinary farmers. The resulting atmosphere of "unrelenting cold nights," where life and death are perilously close, and the people are struggling to survive on the brink of death, encapsulates the specific historical reality of Northeast society. This dire situation, where national contradictions had escalated into the central conflict, is powerfully conveyed and explained through the narrative.

Zhou Libo once remarked on Luo Feng's writing, stating, "Luo Feng has likely either personally suffered at the hands of the enemy or witnessed their brutality firsthand, for he often writes with sorrowful indignation about their cruelty."[1] This observation is undoubtedly accurate. In fact, it was not just Luo Feng, nearly all Northeast writers consciously and passionately depicted the enemy's atrocities with an unrestrained sense of rage. Behind this unrelenting drive to expose such horrors lay an undeniable sense of mission, deeply embedded in the writers' creative pursuits. The sight of bloodstained bayonets served as an unfiltered testament to the true nature of the so-called "Benevolent Rule." Their stark and unembellished narrative serves not only as a direct indictment of oppression but also as a powerful call for the revival of human dignity within the nation, awakening those whose national consciousness has long been numbed. It is precisely this raw and unflinching realism that defines the unique artistic appeal of their works.

It is worth noting that the writers did not portray national conflicts in isolation; rather, they situated them within the broader social context of Northeast China, illustrating the process of their transformation and highlighting the intricate coexistence and entanglement of national and class struggles.

Duanmu Hongliang's novel *Horqin Banner Grassland* sketches a vivid depiction of the evolving class relations in Northeast China on the eve of the Mukden Incident. Centered around the fierce class struggle over land ownership and distribution, the novel contrasts Ding Ning, a landlord and capitalist, with Dashan, a representative of the peasantry. The narrative unfolds to reveal that while the awakened peasants find their path to resistance, the landlord and national bourgeoisie, epitomized by Ding Ning, face inevitable

---

[1] Zhou Libo: *A Retrospective on Novel Writing in 1936—A Year of Abundance*, *Guangming Journal*, No.2, Volume 2, 1937

decline, growing increasingly decadent and ultimately becoming mere pawns of the invading forces. Meanwhile, *Sparks in the Cold Night* focuses on the rampant oppression in occupied rural areas, where national and class exploitation intertwine in a grotesque fusion. *The Field of Life and Death*, on the other hand, does more than expose the political and economic plight of the landless Northeast peasants; it delves deeper into their psychological state, revealing how entrenched feudal forces numb their spirits and dictate their tragic fate. Through this lens, the novel captures a crucial aspect of the era's defining characteristics.

The female writer Xiao Hong, in her works depicting her hometown and childhood, vividly exposes the profound spiritual enslavement and repression inflicted upon the people of Northeast China by feudal traditions—an affliction as insidious as opium. Her sharp critique, infused with deep philosophical and social reflection, is nothing short of astonishing. These elements, subtly woven into a tone tinged with melancholy, are conveyed through meticulous and powerful prose, skillfully orchestrated character destinies, and an underlying emotional depth that evokes profound sympathy and lasting contemplation in her readers. The pure and kind-hearted Aunt Cui (from *March in a Small Town*), yearning for the freedom of love and marriage, departs this world in sorrow; the impoverished student Wang Yaming (from *Hands*), driven by an unquenchable thirst for knowledge, is forced to leave school in anguish; the rural woman Jin Zhi (from *The Field of Life and Death*), struggling under the brutal oppression of patriarchy, desperately searches for a path to survival. In *Tales of Hulan River*, the robust young girl known as the younger daughter-in-law does not merely succumb to her mother-in-law's torment—rather, she is ultimately destroyed by an invisible oppressor, the suffocating grip of feudal ethics, which crushes her spirit before it takes her life. In the long feudal history of Northeast China, generation after generation toiled endlessly—first struggling to survive, then resigning themselves to death—trapped within a rigid and oppressive economic system that not only bound their livelihoods but also confined their minds in a state of stagnation, numbness, and conservatism, creating an atmosphere of suffocating despair. What a bleak yet undeniable reality! Xiao Hong's portrayal of the feudal shackles that crush human nature, suppress the spirit, and distort the soul is so incisive that it seems to pierce through the very fabric of her writing. Yet, even within this grotesque reality, shaped by the long reign of feudal despotism, the reader can still glimpse the flickers of unyielding hearts, hear the faint echoes of resistance and cries for change from the people of Northeast China. Though their voices may be fragile and subdued, they persist, signaling the emergence of a new direction. This spark of idealistic pursuit, like embers glowing in the cold night or radiant stars piercing the darkness, symbolizes the future of Northeast China. The revival and awakening of the human spirit were vividly captured in these works. To understand the overarching aesthetic characteristics of the "Northeastern Writers in Exile" is, in essence, to illuminate the "historical awareness" embedded in their literature from an artistic perspective—an endeavor to grasp the fundamental essence of the era in which these writers lived and created. Lenin once stated, "If we are dealing with a truly great artist, he will inevitably reflect at least certain essential aspects of the revolution in his works." (Lenin, *Leo Tolstoy as the Mirror of the Russian Revolution*). The writers of Northeast China remained faithful to the lives they had experienced, employing a realist approach to depict the unembellished realities of their surroundings. In doing so, they objectively revealed the fundamental characteristics of Northeast society at the time, making their works the most authentic mirror through which to understand that historical era.

II. The Rise of the National Soul

When a culture transforms into a profound tradition of a nation, becoming a symbol of its cultural spirit and flowing through the very blood of its people, it settles into the long, continuous river of national history, becoming an inseparable part of the nation's identity, eternally preserved.

Amid the blending of Eastern and Western cultures, literary works that embody the distinct characteristics of a nation inevitably possess greater potential for development, gradually reaching the global stage. The historical significance of the "Northeastern Writers in Exile" stands out precisely in its ability to preserve the cultural spirit of the Chinese nation while simultaneously fostering engagement with world cultures.

The works of Northeast writers notably emphasize the traditional qualities of the Chinese people, such as resilience, independence, and resistance to foreign invasion, traits that lie at the very core of the nation's character, embodying its "soul."

As Russian critic Belinsky once remarked, "A person is first and foremost a person of their nation." The works of Northeast writers do not merely serve as an exhibition of regional customs or folklore; instead, they intricately weave together the specific lifestyles and historical contexts of Northeast China, thereby highlighting the profound essence of the Northeast "person."

In these works, bloodshed becomes a backdrop for deep reflection, with suffering and hardship giving birth to resistance. As the contradictions between national and class struggles reached a boiling point, the inevitable outcome was the intensifying resistance of the Northeast people, eventually culminating in a powerful wave for national liberation.

In their works, characters who embark on the path of resistance are ubiquitous. There are early awakened farmers, such as Da Shan (*Horqin Banner Grassland*), Lu Youxiang (*Sparks in the Cold Night*), Jing Quanlong (*The Past Years*), and Li Qingshan (*The Field of Life and Death*), who rise against the dual oppression of class and nation; there are also strong soldiers actively engaged in the anti-Japanese guerrilla forces, such as Chen Zhu and

Tie Ying (*Village in August*); and there are hesitant, wavering farmers who gradually awaken, like the timid and cautious Er Li Ban, and Zhao San, nicknamed "Good Heart" (*The Field of Life and Death*). The characters in these works are diverse in both personality and identity. There is the warm and kind old aunt (*Life and Death*), the bold and straightforward hunter's daughter, Shui Qinzi (*The Raging Current of the Hunhe River*), the defiant and unyielding peasant woman, Li Qisao (*Village in August*), the foreign fighters who participated in the struggle for the liberation of the Northeast, such as Anna (*Village in August*) and the Korean child Guli (*Children Without a Homeland*), the bandit, Mei Heizi (The Distant Wind and Sand), the young female student, Chun Xiong (*Horqin Banner Grassland*), and the intellectual, Xiao Ming (*Village in August*), among others. These individuals come from different backgrounds and experiences, each with distinct personalities and appearances. Yet, they collectively represent various layers of society under oppression, demonstrating the widespread resistance of the Northeast people. If we set aside their different origins, personalities, initial motivations for resistance, and methods, we can clearly sense the guiding hand of the era itself. It is the harsh realities of the Northeast region and the surrounding environment that pushed these characters onto the path of resistance, imbuing them with this characteristic of their time.

In portraying this, the writers demonstrate remarkable care and precision, never simply lingering on the superficial aspects of resistance, but instead endeavoring to explore the deeper, more specific facets of the acts of defiance. They aim to reveal the historical significance that underpins such actions, with particular emphasis on illustrating the resilience and unwavering national spirit of the Northeast people. These quiet, steadfast peasants, silently battling fate, are constantly on the brink of collapse under the weight of their suffering, yet they invariably rise again, standing resolute in the face of adversity. This unyielding tenacity becomes a powerful symbol of the enduring character of the Chinese nation.

The writers' portrayal of the inner patriotic sentiments and national spirit of the Northeast people is truly remarkable. In Shu Qun's renowned novel *Children Without a Homeland*, the delicate depiction of two children's patriotic feelings reflects the deep and sincere love for their country that resides in the hearts of the Northeast people. They long for freedom, yearning for the day when the national flag will rise once more. Through the children's psychological journey and their longing for their "motherland," the novel raises a profound question: "What tragic fate awaits those who have lost their homeland?" This powerful theme, coupled with the noble national spirit, deeply resonates with readers, stirring their emotions. As Zhou Yang aptly commented, it "expresses national sentiment in a way that has never been portrayed so intensely in previous works." In Duan Mu Hongliang's short story *Why Grandpa Won't Eat Sorghum Porridge*, an elderly man, on the anniversary of the Mukden Incident, refuses to eat sorghum porridge, choosing to fast as a form of protest. The protagonist quotes a famous line by the Southern Song poet Lu You: "The tears of the exiles dry in the barbarian's dust; They gaze to the south, awaiting the king's return, with hope and trust." The profound and tragic patriotism expressed by this elderly character carries deep emotional weight. Moreover, works such as Ma Jia's *Family Letter*, Lin Jue's *The Unyielding Child*, Li Huiying's *Homesickness*, and Shu Qun's long poem *In the Hometown* seem to speak in unison, expressing the sorrow and suffering of a lost nation, as well as the poignant emotions of patriotism and homesickness, leaving readers moved and deeply affected.

In Xiao Jun's short story *Cherry Blossoms*, there is a pivotal scene where the daughter, Lili, is about to travel from Harbin to Tianjin. Before her departure, her father repeatedly reminds her with a sense of urgency: "You are returning to our homeland! We are Chinese! ... Do not ever say 'Manchukuo' again, for that would invite ridicule. Instead, tell them you are from Northeast China... The three northeastern provinces were violently seized by the Japanese with their bayonets and cannons." Each of these words carries profound significance, rooted deeply in the specific historical and social context of Northeast China at that time. These reminders encapsulate the unique psychological state and identity of the people from this region, vividly reflecting their resolute national pride and their refusal to be associated with the "Manchukuo" identity. It is this fierce sense of nationalism that lies at the very heart of the literature of "Northeastern Writers in Exile."

In expressing this emotion, the "Northeastern Writers in Exile" are particularly attentive to tracking and portraying the inner lives of ordinary characters. They focus on illustrating these characters' personalities through their fates, depicting the gradual process of their spiritual awakening. This progression in perspective is what makes their works so intriguing.

These writers excel at shaping characters by observing the ordinary lives of people, focusing on the most subtle actions and psychological changes. In *Village in August*, the young farmer Tang Laogeda, even amidst life-and-death moments on the battlefield, remains preoccupied with thoughts of his lover, and the inner hesitation and conflict he experiences are portrayed in exquisite detail. Another young farmer, Tian Lao Ba, while also harboring thoughts of resisting the Japanese, lies on his bed pondering, only to delay his decision due to his concern for his "small child" and "beloved wife," deciding to "wait a little longer."

In the novel *The Field of Life and Death*, there is a brilliant depiction of the farmer Er Li Ban's decision to join the anti-Japanese struggle. He is homeless, unemployed, with nothing but an old goat as his only possession. It is only by killing this goat, his last attachment, that he can resolve to resist. As Er Li Ban raises his knife "higher than his head," the knife falls but does not strike the goat. Instead, it "cuts down a small tree." When "the old goat walks over and scratches at his legs," he finally loses his last ounce of courage. He hands the goat over to a neighbor for care, reluctantly leaving. On the road to fight the Japanese, his steps are filled with hesitation, almost as if he turns back three times before continuing. Through this detail, where Er Li Ban raises the knife high only for it to fall helplessly, Xiao Hong vividly portrays the characteristic hesitation of Northeast farmers when they are pushed toward resistance. Their self-sufficient economy and small-scale farming bind them to family, land, and livestock, making their resistance hesitant, which reflects the true emotional turmoil felt by most Northeast farmers in the early stages of the occupation. The work not only suggests that the desire for resistance was shared by the people of Northeast China and that they would inevitably embark on this path, but also illustrates their internal conflict. This duality is evident in their ambivalence towards the anti-Japanese struggle when it first begins. In this way, the novel accurately captures the unique characteristics and ideological trajectory of the Northeast farmers in this specific historical context, while also offering the author’s reflection on the fate of the farmers in reality. In Luo Feng’s novel *The Seventh Pit*, the cobbler Geng Da, under the pressure of the Japanese invaders, digs six pits in which he buries his own fellow countrymen (including his own uncle). During this time, he is passive and tolerant, lacking the courage to directly confront the enemy. However, when he learns that the seventh pit is prepared for him, he finally awakens and resists, bravely striking the enemy's head with a shovel, which reflects the common fear, numbness, and submissive psychological state of urban civilians when the city first falls to the enemy, which is a rational and understandable response.

Geng Da’s resistance, though somewhat delayed, was ultimately inevitable. This plot intricately intertwines personal rebellion with the broader theme of national liberation, imbuing the story with profound symbolism. The portrayal of the people of Northeast China and the exploration of their inner lives are rich with historical depth, offering not only a compelling and authentic narrative but also representing the essence of the novel’s realism.

A great literary work, at its core, uncovers the deep, hidden currents of historical aesthetic trends within the hearts of the people by observing and analyzing the lives, fates, and souls of ordinary individuals. As Russian critic

Dobrolyubov said, "The measure of a writer or a particular work's value, we believe, is how much they express the aspirations of a certain era and a certain nation" (Dobrolyubov, *A Ray of Light in the Dark Kingdom*). When a writer of a nation expresses the history and life of that nation using the unique emotional and aesthetic approaches of their people, and when their creation aligns with the aesthetic emotions and resonates with the hearts of the people, they become a writer of the times, a son of the people, and will create exceptional, immortal works.

The works of the "Northeastern Writers in Exile" demonstrate a remarkable penetrating insight into the soul and essence of the Chinese nation. Within the traditional character of the Chinese people lies a contradiction: on one hand, it inherits certain passive aspects of Chinese traditional culture, manifesting as a closed, self-sufficient, and self-centered system. It praises the doctrine of the mean, advocates moderation and avoiding extremes, acknowledges the reality of existence, and shies away from struggle, which represents a self-regulating, conflict-diminishing temperament. On the other hand, the Chinese nation has always been characterized by a strong tradition of resistance, displaying justice and righteousness in the face of evil, with the heroic spirit of being unyielding and unbending as its core. Both of these contrasting aspects are clearly felt in the creations of the "Northeastern Writers in Exile." They historically bear the burden of the nation's traditional culture, while simultaneously daring to confront life head-on, dissecting the national character. In navigating the contradictions of social life and the national psyche, they have recognized the weakness in their national character and endeavored to present a multifaceted and nuanced portrayal of it. They inherit tradition but also dare to break from it; they remain faithful to reality yet possess a forward-thinking historical consciousness. Because of this, the spiritual temperament of their works is rich and complex, not only marked by a strong sense of the era but also imbued with a long-standing historical awareness, leaving traces of historical continuity. With a broad historical perspective, they portray the profound and far-reaching history of a nation and showcase the tragic heroism of the people. These elements constitute the spiritual essence of the "Northeastern Writers in Exile."

III. The Deep Exploration of the Writer's Individual Power

When engaging with a piece of literature, the most fascinating aspect lies in unraveling the mystery behind the creation of such art. How does this clear and untainted artistic stream flow so effortlessly from the writer's pen? The writer's creative process can be likened to a mysterious realm, where the allure of artistic imagery is not merely born from life itself, but from the writer's deep and rich artistic personality.

Literary works have a direct impact on the human soul, as they engage the reader's senses through the act of reading, triggering an aesthetic experience. Consequently, these works serve to express the inner workings of the human mind and the emotions that define it, conveying the writer's subjective emotional experience. This artistic personality, which springs from the writer's own perspective, exudes an irresistible vitality that infuses the work with immense energy, captivating and influencing the reader's heart. When the reader's soul is stirred, it is, in essence, the writer's individual power that conquers and resonates within them.

The works of the "Northeastern Writers in Exile" clearly embody this dynamic and compelling individual power. They stand out for two key qualities: their immediate reflection of the era and their deep integration with the writer's own life experiences.

Through these works, one can always sense the pulse of the times, as the writer's fervent emotions—his love for life, his devotion to the people—flow freely, harmonizing with his creative individuality as it delves deeply into the era, producing a resonant and harmonious expression of artistic creation.

In his commentary on *Village in August*, Mr. Lu Xun remarked, "The author's blood, the lost sky, land, suffering people, and even the lost lush grass, sorghum, crickets, and mosquitoes, all become tangled together, unfolding vividly in front of the reader's eyes in a brilliant red." (Lu Xun, *Preface to Tian Jun's "August in the Village"*) This passage profoundly captures the echo of the times reflected in the work. In *The Field of Life and Death*, Xiao Hong poignantly describes the solemn ceremony where the farmers pledge to resist Japan: "The cries pierce the heart, falling like sharp wedges into everyone's chest. A wave of intense sorrow sweeps over the bowed heads, and the pale blue sky seems on the verge of collapsing!" This heartrending cry of the people echoes the spirit of the times. Similarly, while in exile in Beiping, Ma Jia's novel *Family Letter* vividly expresses his longing for his loved ones. He imagines his younger brother, wondering, "Is he still as lively as before? Does he still run and jump in the grassy fields? Now, the homeland must be experiencing another spring, though the northern climate is a bit delayed. I believe the entire Northeast Plain has turned into a sea of green... At this moment, my brother must be singing; his voice is so light, with a melody that gently stirs through the grasslands. His innocent soul is entirely melted by the power of nature...He doesn't know that many of the fields have already been abandoned..."

As one reads the above descriptions, an emotional response inevitably stirs within the reader, but can we truly distinguish whether this effect arises from the writer's artistic temperament or the influence of the era? Perhaps it is best to acknowledge that both elements are intertwined, or perhaps a fusion of the two. Whether it is the "lost sky, land," or the "lush grass, sorghum, crickets, mosquitoes, all tangled together," or the imagery of "bowed heads, the pale blue sky on the brink of collapse," or even the bittersweet thoughts of "Has the hometown grass turned green again?" and the tender vision of the brother softly singing on the grass, all of these vivid natural images, deeply imbued with the writer's strong inner vitality, are carefully captured. They are blended with the writer's overflowing creative personality, interwoven with passion, and subtly tinged with the undercurrents of the era's backdrop, culminating in a kind of moving allure that resonates with the reader.

A talented writer's artistic individuality is often imbued with emotional hues, and their emotions are frequently in a state of readiness, poised to be awakened. When an external experience triggers a specific link in this emotional chain, igniting the desire to create, the writer's unique artistic character fully emerges. The period of life with which a writer is most familiar—where their emotional accumulation is the deepest—often forms the most solid foundation for their artistic preparation. Works set against this backdrop tend to best showcase the writer's creative essence, representing the pinnacle and culmination of their lifelong literary achievements.

After the Mukden Incident, the literary creations of the "Northeastern Writers in Exile" surged forth like an unbridled torrent, flowing ceaselessly like a great river carving its path through the land, embodying a vigorous and unrestrained creative spirit. The key to this artistic outpouring lies in the depth and intensity of their lived experiences during that turbulent period. Their works emerged from the most deeply felt, emotionally charged, and profoundly rooted chapter of their personal histories, where their artistic sensibilities were sharpened and their creative impulses found their fullest expression.

These writers were all natives of Northeast China, having grown up immersed in its landscapes and deeply intertwined with its social fabric. Many of them had firsthand experience under the puppet regime during the period of Japanese occupation. Writers such as Xiao Jun, Xiao Hong, Shu Qun, and Luo Feng lived in Harbin for an extended period under enemy rule before eventually leaving. Others, like Ma Jia, Li Huiying, and Duanmu Hongliang, returned to the Northeast even after initially fleeing the south of the Great

Wall, seeking to reconnect with their homeland and further enrich their understanding of life under occupation. These lived experiences proved to be invaluable. More importantly, the emotional wounds inflicted by the humiliation and anguish of the Mukden Incident, along with the subsequent hardships of exile, profoundly shaped their creative consciousness. When they bid farewell to their homeland and parted from their loved ones; when they tasted the bitterness of a lost nation and witnessed firsthand the gradual transformation of Northeast China into a distorted colonial state; when they wandered through the south of the Great Wall, only to be confronted with the Nationalist government's passive resistance policy, where many continued their indulgent, apathetic existence, deaf to the gunfire echoing from the north of the Great Wall—what must have been their state of mind? What anguish must they have endured? As Luo Feng vividly described, "I am nothing more than a crow driven from my homeland by disaster, now flying into this so-called 'peaceful world' using my coarse, grating voice to pour out years of pent-up suffering." This deep sorrow and indignation, this uniquely harrowing experience of exile, imbued their works with a rich emotional intensity unmatched by their counterparts from the south of the Great Wall. For these young writers in their twenties, the turbulence and upheaval of just a few years were more than enough to equal decades of a mundane, uneventful existence. Combined with their unconventional writing styles, these experiences shaped their distinct literary identities.

Chapter 3 The Shuddering Soul of Art

I. A Unique Form of "Recollection Writing"

The most renowned works of "Northeastern Writers in Exile" were predominantly created after these writers had fled to the south of the Great Wall, relying on their recollections of past experiences and life in Northeast China. This form of "literature of recollection" became a distinctive artistic characteristic that defined their creative style.

This distinctive feature of "recollection" in literary creation is something commonly shared by writers in their artistic endeavors, yet in the case of the "Northeastern Writers in Exile," it takes on a unique form that sets their work apart. As a segment of life they personally experienced, it may have already passed, but as an ongoing reality, particularly in its emotional accumulation and lingering resonance, it has not truly faded but instead continues to unfold. When these writers created their works in the south of the Great Wall, the very life they depicted, especially the resistance of the Northeastern people against Japanese aggression, was still unfolding with great intensity, and as their emotions extended, surged, and deepened through contemplation on life, they imbued their works with even greater inspirational force. By transforming the historical life they had once experienced, by shaping that once-dynamic existence into the seemingly static form of literary expression, they paradoxically ensured that life itself remained in motion and development, allowing their recollection and experience of it to undergo continuous enrichment and expansion.

Many outstanding writers, both in China and abroad, ultimately present the historical life they have experienced in the form of literary works, often after a varying lapse of time. The German poet Heinrich Heine, in his essay On "*Love for the Fatherland*", once wrote, "The essence of spring can only be truly recognized in winter, and the finest poems of May can only be composed behind the warmth of a fireplace." In this vivid metaphor, he articulates a fundamental principle of literary creation. Although a writer immerses himself deeply in life, a full understanding of its significance is not easily attained, for he is often unable to immediately and accurately grasp the entirety of the values contained within his experiences. Instead, he must undergo a process of reconsideration and reevaluation, a process of "recollection" in which the "images of memory" in his mind are recreated, the emotions that have settled over time are re-experienced and contemplated, and only through this act of artistic reconstruction can the resulting work achieve a greater power to move its readers and delve more profoundly into the essence of life itself.

As the writer's understanding of the essence of things gradually deepens, the "images of memory" that originally existed in his mind also undergo corresponding changes, enabling him to depict objective reality with greater vividness and authenticity. Hegel regarded the phenomenon of memory as an indispensable factor in artistic creation and an essential stage in the creative process. He stated:

"This creative activity also relies on a strong memory, allowing one to retain the richly varied images of this colorful world...The artist must immerse himself in this material and establish an intimate connection with it." (*Aesthetics*, Hegel)

When an artist immerses himself in the rich materials of the real world and establishes an intimate connection with them, what serves as the link between them? It is memory alone. For a writer, recollection is not merely a passive psychological function but rather an active and creative intellectual process. With the passage of time, this memory becomes thoroughly intertwined with the writer's artistic imagination, merging into a unified whole and giving rise to more complete and exquisite artistic creations. The renowned playwright Stanislavski once said:

"Time, being the finest filter, serves as the best purifier for emotions that have been recalled and experienced. Moreover, time is considered the most marvelous artist, not only cleansing but also transforming memories into something poetic. Due to this unique characteristic of memory, even the most tragic realities and the harshest naturalistic experiences, after a certain period, become more beautiful and artistic. "(*Stanislavski Collected Works*, Stanislavski)

The creative works of the "Northeastern Writers in Exile" exemplify this process. The depiction of Northeastern social life in their works remains as harsh, tragic, and solemn as ever, interwoven with cries of blood and tears; yet, what the reader feels in their soul is the cultivation of artistic beauty. It can be said that these works are no longer simple portrayals of the original reality of life, but have instead become "life" in the writer's memory, having been "poetized" by the writer. They originate from the truth of life, yet transcend it; they now encompass the writer's hopes for the future and his belief in the bright prospects of the Northeast, blending in a significant degree of the writer's experiences of life in the interior. Therefore, this has transformed into a Northeastern life that has been spiritualized, poetized, and made more truly authentic.

When Duanmu Hongliang wrote *Horqin Banner Grassland*, he had already reached adulthood. However, every blade of grass, every tree, the vast, flat plains, and the dense willows and thatched huts depicted in the book all shine with the unforgettable memories of his childhood and youth spent in his hometown. Ma Jia's *Sparks in the Cold Night* and his later novel *Chronicles of the Northern Lands* are filled with the captivating scenery of the Liao River Plain, a landscape that had influenced him deeply since his childhood, with the memories of his early years continuing to shape his writing. In his essay collection Local Collection, Li Huiying fondly recalls the small, remote Jinjiatun village. During the severe winter, he writes that "the lips and whiskers of the mules and horses were covered in thick layers of white frost," and how "the coachman's whip would always crack sharply and crisply," cutting through the vast expanse of the sky. He remembers how, on snowy days, he and the children would catch sparrows, sneak into gardens to steal cucumbers, or roast beans, each memory brimming with unspoken delight. These recollections, filled with nostalgia, are common in the works of the "Northeastern Writers in Exile." A true artist, regardless of where he finds himself or how many hardships he endures, carries the memories of his childhood with him, particularly the emotional ones, which do not fade over time. These memories often permeate his lifetime of creations, shaping the style and distinctive characteristics of his works.

The most convincing example of this can be found in Xiao Hong's works. Her novels *The Field of Life and Death*, *Tales of Hulan River*, and *March in a Small Town* are all profoundly marked by the imprint of her childhood memories, transforming into a form of "reminiscence literature" that has been "poetized." The scenery of the northern small town of Hulan, with its distinct atmosphere, along with characters such as the stubborn Feng Mogan, the cheerful but ultimately tortured younger daughter-in-law, and figures like Yueying and her grandfather, all of them, smiling, crying, and calling out, seem to approach us, and their fates deeply touch our hearts. Due to the passage of time before these memories are recalled, the emotional depth in Xiao Hong's works becomes particularly intense, as if they are bathed in a golden glow, shining brightly and radiating Xiao Hong's unique artistic personality, which is clearly illustrated in the "Epilogue" of *Tales of Hulan River*:

"The butterflies, grasshoppers, and dragonflies in the garden may still be there year after year, or perhaps now the place is completely desolate."

"The small cucumbers and large melons may still be planted every year, or maybe they have disappeared altogether."

"Does the morning dew still fall on the flowerpot stand? Does the midday sun still shine on the tall sunflowers...?"

Xiao Hong seems to have become lost in her boundless daydreams and longing for her hometown, casually writing lyrical verses of nostalgia. Within these words, there is a faint sense of homesickness, but more prominently, there is a deep love for her hometown and a yearning for the future, all shining with the author's inner pursuit of beauty. Many people love reading Xiao Hong's works and marvel at her artistic talent, yet few realize that it is the distinctive emotional memories formed in her childhood that serve as the foundation for her unique style. This form of "reminiscence literature" is full of genuine emotions and longings, possessing a timeless charm.

The relationship between stable visual memories and the emotional experiences stored by the writer is clearly proportional. The deeper the emotional experience of the memory, the stronger and more vivid the visual memory becomes, and vice versa. Although the "Northeastern Writers in Exile" fled to the south of the Great Wall after the Mukden Incident, leaving behind their lives in the Northeast, the pain of losing their homeland, the anger of not being able to resist the Japanese invasion, and the various stimuli of life in the interior constantly deepened and enriched their memories of their hometowns and childhood. The richness and freshness of these memories, stored in their hearts, remained vibrant and only grew stronger and more intense over time. Duanmu Hongliang, when discussing his writing of *The Melancholy of Cilu Lake*, said, "In the novel, the scenery I write about is all based on what was there at the time, and the story is written according to the things that happened there, because I was moved. And now, thinking back, it still moves me."[1] The key point here is his statement, "I was moved" and "it still moves me." The abundant emotional soil nurtures the radiant flowers of vivid memories, truly evoking admiration.

II. The Power of Emotional Laws

[1] Duanmu Hongliang: *Preface to Selected Novels of Duanmu Hongliang*, included in *Selected Novels of Duanmu Hongliang*, Hunan People's Publishing House, 1981.

In the process of transforming the reality of life into artistic reality, the writer's inner emotional factors hold a significant position. As Leo Tolstoy said, art is "the conscious transmission of emotions one has personally experienced to others, so that others, moved by these emotions, can experience them as well" (*What is Art?*, Leo Tolstoy).

The creation of artistic imagery, from the transformation of the aesthetic object to the aesthetic experience, cannot be separated from the materialization of the writer's subjective emotions. Artistic emotions must both align with the common-sense logic and rationality of life, while also deviating from them in certain ways. Emotions know no bounds, and some things that appear irrational in everyday life can feel profoundly authentic within an artistic work. The key here is emotional resonance. When a writer's emotions "move into" the reader's heart, they often stimulate the reader to feel the same emotions. At certain points of deep emotional exchange, they communicate with one another, thereby creating a "shared emotion." The works of the "Northeastern Writers in Exile" were able to have such a significant impact and gain wide praise precisely because they resonated with the readers' sense of patriotism, concern for the people, and the urgency of national salvation. They struck a deep chord in the readers' hearts, triggering a "shared emotion." This triggering of "shared emotion" occurs in two main ways.

1. The Subtle and Pervasive Method

Pervasion, in this context, refers to the process by which the writer, through artistic imagination and expression, transforms their unique emotional experience of an objective entity into a vibrant feeling, naturally infusing it into the object, making it more vivid and intense. During this process, the objective entity becomes a life carrier imbued with emotional qualities. It is evident that pervasion is realized through the mechanism of empathy. The subtle nature of the emotions in the works of Northeastern writers and their ability to permeate the reader often trigger a corresponding echo of emotions in the readers, whose feelings are similarly awakened and mirrored.

Earlier, we mentioned a passage from the "Epilogue" of Xiao Hong's *Tales of Hulan River*. The small cucumbers, the large melons, the morning dew, and the midday sun are all woven into the writer's musings and recollections, undoubtedly conveying some kind of sentiment. What does it make us think of? It seems as though no one can clearly express it, yet everyone might offer some interpretation: is it a reflection on their own hometown, their own childhood, or perhaps a sigh in response to Xiao Hong's life and fate, which then leads them into their own reverie? The reader's emotional response is vague, blurry, and varies from person to person. However, one thing is certain: it connects with the author's inner emotions, intertwining through a subtle, unconscious permeation. Now, let's look at a passage from writer Li Huiying's essay *Nostalgia for My Hometown*:

"After my grandfather passed away, my longing for him grew, just as the further I am from home, the more I think of my hometown. In my mind, from childhood to middle age, and even into old age, I will always believe that Jinjiatun Village is the most beautiful village, that Jinjiatun Village is the most perfect poem... The local mountain songs, though crude, have forever taken root in my heart. Not only is "the moon brighter in my hometown," but even the sun of my hometown is warmer than elsewhere. The slopes of my hometown, the flocks of sheep, the rivers, the fields of grain... These and more, unknowingly, resurface during the midnight hours, bringing with them the weight of deep homesickness."

This paragraph, much like the earlier excerpt from Xiao Hong, conveys a shared melody of longing for one's hometown. Both writers capture life forms with vivid imagery, such as small cucumbers, large melons, midday sunflowers, or the crude mountain songs, slopes, flocks of sheep, and the moon. The writers infuse their works with a personal, emotionally charged "inner drive," transforming these objective entities into symbols of "hometown." During the reader's engagement with the text, the writer's emotions subtly enter the reader's heart alongside the concrete artistic images.

This process is akin to gentle rain seeping into the soil, quietly nurturing new life. At the same time, because the writers are still living in a state of displacement and exile, their real-life experiences amplify their feelings of homesickness, making them even more intense and uncontrollable. Once expressed, these emotions become all the more moving. This method of emotional transmission through subtle pervasion is highly effective in conveying artistic impact.

2. The Surging Outpouring Method

The representations of the image memories in the writer's mind can change due to their new environment and psychological state. When combined with new memories, these representations take on more vivid emotional hues. As years pass and the writer's understanding of life deepens, these memories are stored more profoundly, yet their expression becomes even more intense. The writer's emotions are strengthened by reason, which in turn makes them more profound and expansive.

The northeastern writers, exiled to the south of the Great Wall amidst a time of profound turmoil and upheaval, enduring the relentless hardships of displacement, found themselves overwhelmed by deep inner grief and frustration. Within this new, unfamiliar social and living environment, their thoughts and emotions, now amplified by their circumstances, became exceptionally intense and uninhibited. Their ideals crystallized with increasing clarity, their voices resonated with greater power, and their romanticism, infused with an undeniable urgency, became even more striking. This raw and unrestrained outpouring of emotion, thus, emerged as yet another defining hallmark of their creative expression.

In *A Retrospective on My Poetry Creation*, Mu Mutian passionately lamented, "The people of the Northeast face daily massacres. Bombs are dropped on their heads every day from the radio. Artillery shells bombard them every day... So, what are we poets to do with our hearts?" He felt himself trapped in a state of deep sorrow and melancholy. His anxious heart could no longer be calmed; the only way to bring balance to his troubled mind seemed to be by singing out the emotions in his heart, by expressing through poetry the painful reality faced by his fellow Northeasterners. He resolved to "lower my head to witness the suffering of the oppressed people... to write out their desolation" (*To the Young Friends of the Northeast,* Mu Mutian). The poet sang:

Friend, time comes day by day,
Friend, humanity must change the way.
Friend, no longer be a tool to use,
Friend, against our enemies, we must choose to bruise!
(*Here Comes the Grayish-white Dawn Again*, Mu Mutian)

On the third day after the *August 13th Incident*, he wrote in *The Total Mobilization of the Nation*:

On this earth, let oppressed nations roar,
Now's the time to reclaim the Northeast's shore,
Strike the thieves where they nest and hide,
Roar, China, for now the time's your guide!

In *To Hui*, the poet's emotions grow more intense:

Hui! Please, call out loudly to Lili:
"Father! Give me one more bowl of rice,
I'll fight the Japanese devils alone, and pay the price!"

Such an outpouring of emotion, expressed so directly, can only be uttered by a profound poet. The highly influential "recitation poet" Gao Lan and playwright Sai Ke, both stand as flag bearers of the "Northeastern Writers in

Exile" in the genre of passionate, anthemic calls. Gao Lan's poems, *My Home is in Heilongjiang* and *The Cry of the Lost Daughter Sophie*, both carry a bold romantic spirit, widely recited among the people in the interior during the Anti-Japanese War. The theme of Sai Ke's *East Road Line* is unmistakable: "Rise, the Chinese nation under the iron hooves!" In his widely spread play *Thirty Million Refugees*, a fervent national spirit rises:

Crimson blood reflects the blazing sun,
Surging with power, revenge begun.
We are exiles from the Black River's shore,
Returned from prisons, bound no more.

The tyrant's iron hooves crush hill and stream,
Imperial cannons shatter the dream.
The sky is torn by hands of sin,
Storms of blood and war begin.

....

The weight of these words are so powerful, so unrestrained! The hearts of thirty million exiled Northeasterners beat like urgent war drums, their voices rising in a soaring anthem, striking a chord deep within the souls of countless Chinese. This resounding "Roar, China"-style outcry, solemn and majestic, carries an air of heroic tragedy, urging a sense of historical duty while unleashing an unyielding, masculine passion.

Echoing this same spirit are Shu Qun's long poem *In the Hometown* and Ma Jia's *The Fire Sacrifice*. Both share a kindred emotional tone, with forceful language, a rapid and rhythmic pulse, and an overtly radical stance. Their torrential outpouring of emotion crashes down like a mighty flood, leaving an indelible impression on all who hear it.

III. The Vivid Essence of Regional Identity

Many of the "Northeastern Writers in Exile" infused their works with a deep affection for their homeland, painting a rich portrait of the region's distinct natural landscapes and cultural customs. The striking scenery of the northern frontier and the deep-rooted rustic charm became captivating features of their literary creations, standing out particularly in some of their most outstanding works.

In the northern reaches of Manchuria, the bitter cold, vast expanses of ice, and snow-covered landscapes shape a uniquely Northeastern aesthetic—a frozen tableau that defines the region. The opening of *Tales of Hulan River* paints this picture vividly:

"After the harsh winter has sealed up the land, the earth's crust begins to crack and split. From south to north, from east to west; from a few feet to several yards in length; anywhere, anytime, the cracks run in every direction. As soon as harsh winter is upon the land, the earth's crust opens up."

"The severe winter weather splits the frozen earth."

In just a few lines, the cracks in the earth vividly convey the bitter cold of Northeastern winters. Now, let's look at the depiction of the icy landscape:

The people of my hometown all understand that until spring arrives in March, not even the magic of the gods could disperse the endless stretch of snow-covered mountains and rivers.

As soon as the "Great Snow" season sets in, every river and stream freezes over, their surfaces sealed beneath layers of ice. Night and day, the ice thickens, growing stronger with each passing moment. Within ten days or so, the frozen surface becomes so solid that even a two-ton truck can cross it with ease. (*Ice, Deep Winter, Bitter Cold*, Li Huiying)

The thick, unmelting snow of an entire winter and the solid ice covering the land are unique to the Northeast. Even the arrival of spring carries a distinct regional character. It comes and goes in a fleeting moment, so brief and hurried that one can hardly grasp its presence:

"Before the winter snow has fully melted away, summer is already upon us..."

"A poplar tree that seemed completely bare just yesterday suddenly bursts forth with golden buds today. By the third day, delicate green leaves, as if carefully pasted onto the branches by hand, tremble in the breeze." (*The Past Years*, Xiao Jun)

The scenes depicted by these writers not only exude the distinct atmosphere of Northeast China but also carry traces of their childhood experiences, infused with their unique emotional connections to the landscape. Many writers placed great emphasis on capturing the customs of rural northeastern life and the deeply ingrained superstitions of local farmers such as spirit-calling rituals, yangko dances, temple fairs, and river lantern festivals. In *The Past Years*, the landlord Yang Luozhong's grand birthday celebration; *Sparks in the Cold Night*, the slow, measured recitation of superstitious proverbs by the yin-yang master; and Xiao Hong's vivid, joyous, and lyrical depiction of river lanterns drifting along the Hulan River. All these draw directly from the daily lives of the lower-class people of Northeast China. These rich portrayals weave together a vibrant tapestry of folk customs, further enhanced by the writers' skillful use of lively, regionally flavored language, adding a unique artistic charm to their works.

The depiction of Northeast China's regional colors in these writers' works is far from delicate and idyllic pastoral poetry. Instead, it encompasses a wealth of social content, reflecting the realities of the times and standing in stark contrast to purely nostalgic literature. Through vivid portrayals of regional characteristics, their works emphasize the spirit of the era. This deliberate focus on intertwining regional identity with historical consciousness is a defining feature of the "Northeastern Writers in Exile" and their approach to literary creation.

In Ma Jia's *Sparks in the Cold Night*, when the young farmer Lu Youxiang fled from Shenyang and returned home, he found his family living in extreme poverty:

"Leaning against the doorway was a simple stove, its hearth filled with a soft heap of sorghum ash, thick as if it had accumulated for a long time. Scattered bits of dried manure were stuffed into a dung basket..."

"Cold winds seeped through the cracks in the window, making the dim oil lamp flicker constantly. Its weak glow occasionally cast light on the kang bed, revealing a tattered, patchy mat, then shifted to the wall where a set of harnesses hung. A half-filled sieve of millet sat beneath the shadow of the beam, barely visible. Frost clung to the walls and window paper, exuding a chilling, bone-deep coldness."

This is a true depiction of the living conditions of an ordinary Northeast Chinese peasant under the rule of the Japanese puppet regime after the Mukden Incident. Leaning against the doorway is a stove, and on the heated brick kang bed lies a "tattered, patchy mat." "Cold winds seeped through the cracks in the window," and "Frost clung to the walls and window paper" These descriptions vividly capture the specific features of rural houses in Northeast China so shabby and bleak that they powerfully evoke the atmosphere of the era. The social causes behind this poverty-stricken state are self-evident. It is precisely for this reason that Lu Youxiang sharply revealed the reality of such a life: "Ever since the establishment of 'Manchukuo,' even just the official taxes alone have been unbearable for poor households." How could destitute farmers "possibly survive"? The historical backdrop and the regional atmosphere have become inseparably intertwined.

The language of "Northeastern Writers in Exile" often carries a distinct regional flavor of Northeast China. Many writers directly incorporate the spoken language of Northeast farmers, adding vivid color to their works. Imagine the striking and magnificent scenes depicted in their writings: the folk customs of the border town of Aihui, the charm of Hulan Town, the struggles of farmers on the Horqin Grassland, the hardships of villagers along the Liaohe River, the distant echoes of bandit gunfire in the wind and sand, the anti-Japanese banners deep in the dense forests of the Greater Khingan Mountains, the sweeping snowstorms over the Songliao Plain, and the weary footsteps of starving youths on the streets of Harbin... Reading these works, one seems to be transported onto the land of the North, and enchanted by its mesmerizing landscapes, heartbroken for the tormented compatriots, and praying for their hopes. Even after closing the book, the thoughts linger, and the fresh experiences leave a lasting impression.

IV. The Beauty of Strength, The Beauty of Spirit

When examining the overall creative works of "Northeastern Writers in Exile," we can identify several distinct artistic characteristics: First, the color palette of their works is predominantly gray and brown, with a generally cool tone that aligns with the oppressive era and environment of Northeast China. Second, their use of imagery tends to be slow-paced, offering a close-up perspective on the realities of life in the Northeast, which creates a sense of authenticity, psychologically and visually drawing the reader closer to the lived experiences depicted. Third, their works radiate a powerful emotional force and a deep pursuit of beauty, embodying a grand and uplifting beauty of strength and the beauty of the Chinese national spirit.

Duanmu Hongliang's novel *The Ocean of the Land* contains a passage describing the land of Northeast China, which vividly illustrates this beauty of strength and spirit:

"If there were to be a place in the world that was both desolate and vast, then this place, if not the most desolate and the most vast, would surely be one of the most remarkable."

"How open, how far-reaching, how straightforward, how boundless it is! A morning breeze, if it so wished, could blow from one end to the distant horizon without encountering the slightest obstacle along the way. And if by some chance it did meet with a small misfortune midway, if it were blocked by some unexpected protrusion, then surely it would be a clod of earth upturned by the plow, bleeding its dark, rich soil."

This vast, desolate, and boundless expanse, what is it? This "bleeding its dark, rich soil", what does it represent? It is the land of Northeast China. It is the symbol of its history, its society, and its cultural heritage. Writers praise this land, portraying it with the love one has for a mother, evoking in you a sense of grandeur and reverence toward it, which is a beauty that merges profound national sentiment, deep historical significance, and a vivid spirit of the times into one powerful and moving whole.

The desolate wilderness, the snow-covered northern world, the ravages of the Japanese invaders, the sorrowful song in the hearts of the people, everything that has happened and existed in Northeast China is laid bare. When these images, each representing different aspects of reality, merge into one and take shape as a living historical moment, their cold and profound meaning transcends ordinary life and rises to the level of history. The ordinary people of Northeast China move forward within this historical reality. Their footsteps are steady, their resistance is fearless and determined, and their resilience is deeply moving.

On this vast and fertile land, the blood of the people of Northeast China flows silently. It quietly seeps into the soil, nurturing the opening of the buds of the era. Generations of humble and unnoticed Northeasterners have stood tall with stubborn necks. Is this the melancholic yet grand scene recorded in the history books of Northeast China? This is no longer just a beauty in an artistic sense, but a beauty of national spirit, a masculine beauty with historical significance. The birth of this beauty represents a deep insight into the soul of the people of Northeast China, symbolizing a heroic nation that continues to perfect and mature throughout history. Promoting this beauty aligns fundamentally with the mainstream of Chinese cultural spirit and the excellent aesthetic standards of Chinese cultural traditions. Its value, in calling and propelling the spirit of the Chinese nation, is everlasting.

After the smoke of the Mukden Incident's gunfire had barely cleared, on the eve of the nationwide surge of resistance against Japan, a group of writers emerged from the Northeast of China. Their creations were closely linked to the cause of the liberation of the Chinese nation. Their works truthfully reflected the events that unfolded there, giving the people across the country a more genuine understanding of the realities in the Northeast. The events they depicted would soon spread throughout the nation. The reality of the Northeast made people realize that the Chinese nation was at a critical moment of peril, greatly awakening the national consciousness for resistance, which played a vital role in awakening, educating, and inspiring the people. When discussing the impact of Northeast writers' works on Chinese anti-Japanese literature, Zhou Yang said, "The success of *Village in August* and *The Field of Life and Death*, along with the popularity of all works on the theme of anti-Japanese resistance, clearly reflects the inevitable trend of new literature during the peak of the national revolution. Post-war literature naturally developed further along this trend."

The "Northeastern Writers in Exile" occupy a unique position in the history of Chinese literature, who served as a bridge between the old literature of Northeast China and the revolutionary literature of the region and were also an essential link in the transition from the May Fourth New Literature to the national anti-Japanese literature. Moreover, they acted as a bridge for cultural exchange between China and the world.

The works of the "Northeastern Writers in Exile," like the crowing of a rooster before dawn, heralded the arrival of a new era in modern Chinese literary history. They opened a new chapter in the brilliant literary history of the Chinese nation and became the precursor to Chinese anti-war literature, which is their historical significance.

Chapter 4 A Long Way to Go

——The Fate and Literary School of "Northeastern Writers in Exile"

I. Northeast Writers in the Later Stages of the Anti-Japanese War

From 1934 to 1937, the representative works of the "Northeastern Writers in Exile" were gradually published, and the group of these writers had largely taken shape. Their activities were primarily concentrated in two regions: In the south, centered in Shanghai, notable figures included Xiao Hong, Xiao Jun, Li Huiying, Mu Mutian, Shu Qun, Gao Lan, Luo Feng, Bai Lang, Luo Binji, Kong Luosun, Lin Jue, and Ye Lin. In the north, centered in Beiping (now Beijing), notable figures included Duanmu Hongliang (who moved to Shanghai after 1936), Ma Jia, Yang Hui, Yu Yifu, Qiu Qin, Shi Tianshou, and Liu Shude.

During this period, these writers were highly active in their creative endeavors. Although they had no conscious desire to form an organized group or society and never issued manifestos or declarations, the public still viewed them as a cohesive literary collective. This perception was based on their shared regional background and similar thematic focus in their works. The term "Northeast Writers," which emerged at the time, was an objective summary of their common creative characteristics. It can be said that around 1937, the "Northeastern Writers in Exile" had reached maturity and began to establish their place in literary history.

In 1937, the outbreak of the July 7th Incident forced the newly formed group of "Northeastern Writers in Exile" to make yet another critical choice. From that point forward, they became part of the broader nationwide resistance movement against Japan. For Northeast writers, this decision meant continuing to advance with the times and opening up new frontiers for progressive literature from Northeast China. However, as a distinct literary group, the "Northeastern Writers in Exile" began to disintegrate, not only in form but also in substance. From a purely literary perspective, the strengthening of national "anti-Japanese literature" and the arrival of a new literary stage effectively signified the weakening of "Northeast Literature in Exile" and the end of the "Northeastern Writers in Exile" as a historical movement. When the struggle against imperialist aggression was no longer confined to Northeast China but was unfolding on a nationwide scale, when writers from all over the country actively joined this historic battle for national survival, and when "anti-Japanese literature" became the dominant literary theme across China, even the "Northeastern Writers in Exile" themselves voluntarily merged into this great historical tide. At this point, both in terms of literary function and historical significance, the unique social and historical conditions that had sustained the "Northeastern Writers in Exile" began to diminish. Their historical mission was nearing completion, and their natural dissolution was an inevitable and progressive step in alignment with the broader course of history.

After the August 13th Incident in Shanghai, the Northeast writers who had once gathered there gradually retreated to the interior of China. Xiao Jun traveled through Wuhan to Linfen, then moved to Chongqing, and eventually arrived in Yan'an. Xiao Hong stayed for a time in Wuhan and Linfen before going to Chongqing with Duanmu Hongliang, eventually reaching Hong Kong in 1940. Li Huiying also relocated to Hong Kong. Luo Binji first traveled through southern Anhui to Guilin, later moving to Hong Kong before settling again in Guilin. Mu Mutian arrived in Kunming in 1938 and later moved to Guilin in 1942. Luo Feng, Bai Lang, and Shu Qun journeyed inland and eventually reached Yan'an. Ma Jia, after evacuating from Beiping, engaged in wartime propaganda work under Yu Yifu's arrangement before making his way to Yan'an in 1939.

Thus, around 1940 to 1941, after experiencing yet another, even more extensive period of displacement and hardship, most of the "Northeastern Writers in Exile" gradually found relative stability. They became concentrated in three main locations: Yan'an, Guilin, and Hong Kong, maintaining this triangular distribution until the end of the War of Resistance. Among these locations, the largest number of Northeast writers gathered in Yan'an, where they exerted the most significant influence.

The Northeast writers who gathered in Yan'an included Xiao Jun, Luo Feng, Shu Qun, Bai Lang, Sai Ke, Ma Jia, Yu Heiding, Shi Tianshou, and Cai Tianxin. Among the 27 council members of the Yan'an branch of the Chinese Association of Literary and Art Circles for Resisting Enemy, six were from the Northeast. Xiao Jun, besides co-editing the major Yan'an literary magazine *Guyu Journal* with Shu Qun, also served as the editor-in-chief of *Literature Monthly* and the editor of *Lu Xun Research Series*. Luo Feng, in 1939, served as the head of the Propaganda Department of the Chinese Association of Literary and Art Circles for Resisting Enemy. In 1941, he became the first chairman of the Yan'an branch of the Chinese Association of Literary and Art Circles for Resisting Enemy, playing a leading role in Yan'an literary scene.

The Northeast writers in Yan'an once held a small but memorable gathering. On September 18, 1941, the tenth anniversary of the Mukden Incident, nineteen writers jointly published an open letter in the *Literature* section of *Liberation Daily*. The letter, titled "To the Fathers, Brothers, and Sisters of the Four Northeastern Provinces—Also to Literary Workers Across the Country," expressed their deep emotions, stating: "The Northeast people bear a double national humiliation... We have never for a moment forgotten that we are part of the thirty million suffering souls of the Northeast." The nineteen signatories of this letter were: Bai Lang, Bai Xiaoguang (Ma Jia), Shi Guang, Li Lei, Di Geng, Guo Xiaochuan, Ji Jianbo, Gao Yang, Liang Yan, Shi Tianshou, Zhang Ding, Hei Ding, Shu Qun, Lei Jia, Cai Tianxin, Luo Feng, Xiao Jun, Wei Dongming, and Gao Geng. [1]

---

[1] Shen Weiwei: *The Northeast Writers Group during the Yan'an Period*, published in *Journal of Liaoning Normal University (Social Science Edition)*, 1987, No. 1.

These nineteen writers also formed a loosely organized literary group called the "Literary Society for the Mukden Incident." They outlined their mission as follows: "To exchange sentiments about our homeland, study the history, customs, and language of the Northeast, collect various relevant materials to aid in writing, and, when possible, provide reference materials for those concerned with the Northeast." [1]

On January 22, 1942, when news of Xiao Hong's passing in Hong Kong reached Yan'an, a memorial service was specially held by Northeast writers at the Chinese Association of Literary and Art Circles for Resisting Enemy to deeply mourn her untimely death. Additionally, Xiao Jun and Shu Qun each gave accounts of her life and literary contributions.

The Northeast writers in Yan'an were not only active but also developed closer relationships with each other than before. At the same time, the distinctive color of "Northeast Literature in Exile," as a common creative consciousness and a prominent feature, gradually faded, which was a natural result of the new stage of the Anti-Japanese War.

With the change in environment, the creative work of the Northeast writers in Yan'an underwent a significant transformation. The vibrant life in the liberated areas and the Anti-Japanese base areas, the heroic spirit of the Eighth Route Army inspired them, and they threw themselves wholeheartedly into this new struggle. The tone of their works shifted from the previously sorrowful and harsh, from the cold and repressed colors, to the warm and vibrant tones reflecting the Anti-Japanese base areas and the enthusiasm of the army and civilians. The themes of their works also changed, moving from "Northeast" and "exile" to the depiction of life in the liberated areas. In this new living environment, the state of mind of the Northeast writers also changed greatly. They became more open, joyful, and confident. They consciously attached themselves to this bright land, and the sense of political

---

[1] Shen Weiwei: *The Northeast Writers Group during the Yan'an Period*, published in *Journal of Liaoning Normal University (Social Science Edition)*, 1987, No. 1.

identification swept away the loneliness they had felt during their solitary struggles. "Exile" literature began to be replaced by "Liberated Area" literature, and they actively adapted to the new social and historical framework, symbolizing the development of Northeast literature in this new historical stage.

During this period, although Xiao Jun was still writing the novel *The Third Generation*, Bai Lang was working on *Record Outside the Prison*, and Luo Feng was writing *Prisoners from Manchuria*, these creations with Northeast themes were repeatedly interrupted due to their general mismatch with the new struggle environment in the liberated areas at that time. On the other hand, new works reflecting the life in the liberated areas sprang up like bamboo shoots after a rain, growing vigorously. Ma Jia published several works, including *The Recipient of the Honor Flower*, *Encampment*, *General Xiao Ke at Malan*, *Courier Ma Lin*, and *The Interval*, which were sketches from the frontlines. Bai Lang wrote the novel *The Temptation*, Shu Qun penned *Comrade Wu* and *The Fast Track Man*, Hei Ding created *Our Fourth Team* and *The Charcoal Kiln*, Luo Feng wrote *Chasing* and some essays. Lei Jia contributed with *A Type 38 Rifle* and *Evening Song by the Yellow River*, and Sai Ke produced *The Great Chorus of Production*, among many other works that depicted the Eighth Route Army and the life in the liberated areas. Shi Tianshou, Li Lei, Liang Yan, and Zhang Ding also continued to write diligently.

In 1945, on the eve of the victory in the Anti-Japanese War, Ma Jia serialized his novel *The Hutuo River Basin* in the *Liberation Daily* in Yan'an, which was the only long novel serialized in Yan'an at the time. Xiao San, who had just returned from the Soviet Union, was very pleased after reading it and wrote an encouraging letter to Ma Jia. The novel depicts the struggle and life of the military and civilians in the Jin-Cha-Ji Border Area. Undoubtedly, it is the crystallization of the author's firsthand experience in the frontline. Its publication represented the highest literary achievement of the Northeast writers in Yan'an during this period. In a certain sense, it also marked the end of the creative phase of the "Northeastern Writers in Exile".

At the same time, the Northeast writers who had gathered in Hong Kong sparked a wave of "Northeast Literature in Exile" there, with achievements that were impressive. They carried the distinctive features of "Northeastern Writers in Exile" well into the period until Hong Kong fell to Japanese forces in 1941.

Around 1940, Northeast writers in Hong Kong gradually published a series of works imbued with strong local flavors, expressing homesickness and frustration with the world. Xiao Hong's famous novel *Tales of Hulan River* was serialized in *Sing Tao Daily: Zodiac*, and her novel *March in a Small Town* was published in the first issue of *Modern Literature* in July 1941. Additionally, she wrote novels like *Backyard Garden*, *Northern China*, *The Call of the Wilderness*, the long novel *Ma Bole*, a four-act silent drama *The National Soul, Lu Xun*, and *A Letter to Northeast Compatriots in Exile*, entering a period of her most prolific and brilliant creative phase. Duanmu Hongliang published the long novels *The Great River* and *The Great Era* (unfinished), along with the novella *Jiangnan Scenery*. Luo Bingi wrote the novella *The Eastern Battlefield Special Forces* and short stories like *The Farmer's Child* and *The Story of Red Glass*. Li Huiying published a collection of short stories, *Sparks*, as well as several essays.

The overall impression of these works is that the emotions have become more subtle and profound, the character portrayals have reached greater maturity, and the depiction of inner conflicts and psychological depth has become more outstanding. The feeling of homesickness is stronger, and the techniques have grown more sophisticated, while still retaining the distinct and vibrant flavor of Northeast China. Whether it is the melancholic, sorrowful longing for home or the joyful recollection of childhood memories, both are expressed with simplicity and naturalness, without any pretense.

Xiao Hong's creativity reached its peak during this period. Her works

Tales of Hulan River and *March in a Small Town* are emotional masterpieces that deeply move readers. She skillfully portrays the stagnant, numb, and ignorant inner world of Northeast farmers, and relentlessly analyzes the reasons behind the stagnation of old society. When readers come across the scene where a younger daughter-in-law is forcibly pressed into scalding water by her mother-in-law for a bath, ultimately dying from the torment and shock, or when they read about Aunt Cui, who, in pursuit of marital autonomy, destroys her own sick body in futile resistance and dies melancholically, the readers' hearts are inevitably struck by an invisible force. The vibrant life is brutally repressed and stifled, giving rise to a twisted rebellious mentality. The tragic endings of these stories leave readers deeply sorrowful, which is a vivid expression of the writer's own "emotion." Xiao Hong infuses love and hate, joy and sorrow, and melancholy and depression into the soul of her works, touching readers profoundly with her distinct creative personality.

Northeastern writers also published novels in Hong Kong that depicted wartime realities, such as Luo Binji's *The East Battlefield Special Forces* and *Hatred*, Duanmu Hongliang's *The Great River*, and Xiao Hong's *Ma Bole*. These works portray the various people's appearances, joys, and sorrows during the war, with a strong national sentiment and intense realism. They blend with the writers' rural novels, forming the distinctive characteristic of "Northeastern Writers in Exile" in their later works in Hong Kong. These novels enriched the nationwide body of wartime literature and added the final brilliant strokes to the artistic canvas of "Northeastern Writers in Exile."

We cannot assign a precise time to the final disappearance of the "Northeastern Writers in Exile." In general, it was the result of a gradual evolutionary process, one that unfolded alongside the climax of the all-out resistance war, as anti-Japanese literature grew stronger and eventually led to their gradual disbandment and disappearance. The death of the old often marks the birth of new life, where form disappears but the spirit endures. The "Northeastern Writers in Exile" fulfilled their historical role and naturally withdrew from the stage, while the revolutionary literature of Northeast China continued its progress. The Northeastern writers continued to move forward, venturing into a new historical and literary realm, in line with the laws of historical movements. Behind them, a new generation of Northeastern writers was rising, continuing in an unbroken legacy...

II. Literary School of "Northeastern Writers in Exile"

Did the "Northeastern Writers in Exile" form a literary school in the history of modern Chinese literature? The author believes that they did, and in fact, this is a rather important literary school. However, in certain aspects, it may not be considered fully typical or complete.

A literary school often refers to a group of writers with similar or identical ideological tendencies, literary propositions, aesthetic tastes, creative methods, and artistic styles, typically formed during a specific historical period. This group can either be a conscious and intentional collective formed by the writers themselves, or it can be an unconscious formation that is later summarized by later generations. The "Northeastern Writers in Exile" belong to the latter category.

To constitute a literary school, the following three essential factors must be met. Firstly, there must be one or several most influential writers who serve as its representatives, forming a collective group of authors. Secondly, these writers must share fundamentally similar or identical political inclinations, aesthetic tastes, and creative methods. Thirdly, this group of authors must exhibit a certain degree of stylistic similarity in their artistic expression, thereby shaping a distinct literary style characteristic of the school. It is evident that the formation of a literary school is by no means an accidental convergence of writers merely due to shared personal interests or artistic perspectives, nor is it a subjective speculation or arbitrary evaluation imposed by later generations. Rather, it is deeply rooted in profound social and historical contexts as well as class foundations, which can only be traced back to the specific socio-historical environment in which these writers lived. Only when writers are placed within the same historical setting, occupy the same class position, and confront similar social issues, while also sharing broadly consistent political attitudes, cultural backgrounds, and aesthetic ideals, can their works exhibit a certain level of ideological and artistic consistency, thereby forming a distinctive collective characteristic. This consistency, arising from both subjective and objective factors in the creative process, serves as a fundamental prerequisite for the establishment of a literary school.

We can observe that the so-called "Northeastern Writers in Exile" all originated from the land of Northeast China and, for the most part, came from the petty-bourgeois intellectual class, finding themselves in a position of oppression and humiliation at the time. Living in an era of historical turmoil, they personally experienced the catastrophic events of the Mukden Incident, witnessing firsthand the realities of life in Northeast China, the suffering of the people in the occupied areas, the atrocities committed by the Japanese invaders, and the humiliation of national subjugation—experiences that left them with profound and unforgettable impressions. Their emotions of love and hatred, sorrow and joy, were similar, and they shared a common aesthetic perspective of admiration and aversion. Being of similar age, they all made their literary debuts in the early 1930s and went into exile in the south of the Great Wall around the time of the Mukden Incident, undergoing largely the same exilic existence. Following the literary banner of the League of Left-Wing Writers, with Lu Xun as its leading figure, they uniformly adopted a realist approach to creation, earnestly expressing the essence of human life and faithfully portraying the social realities of Northeast China during the 1930s. The subject matter of their works was mostly drawn from the society of Northeast China around the time of the Mukden Incident, focusing on the anti-

Japanese resistance and national salvation as their central themes while demonstrating broadly similar progressive political tendencies and aesthetic preferences. Their writings were all imbued with a strong sense of political consciousness calling for national salvation, consciously raising their voices for the fate of the nation and its people and responding to the pressing reality of the Anti-Japanese War. As a result, they became the conveyors of the dominant historical current and the collective psychological state of the people of their era. Through their participation in class struggles and the cause of national liberation, their ideological orientation gradually inclined toward revolution, leading them to establish a proletarian worldview, and in the end, most of them grew into literary warriors of the proletariat.

We can also observe that their creative works were primarily centered on novels with anti-Japanese themes, in which a strong sense of patriotism was profoundly embedded. Their works generally exhibited an intense awareness of the era, infused with a rich and vivid Northeastern atmosphere and strong regional characteristics, thereby shaping an overall artistic style dominated by solemnity, indignation, and melancholy. The literary creations of the "Northeastern Writers in Exile" had already exerted a significant influence on society at the time and had undoubtedly evolved into a progressive force that launched an assault against the darkness of the social order. Moreover, they indeed once appeared in the form of a collective group—examples of which include the "Northern Manchurian Progressive Writers' Group" in Harbin, the publication of *A Collection of Recent Works by Northeastern Writers* compiled by the editorial board of *Guangming Journal* Semi-Monthly in 1936, and the establishment of the "Literary Society for the Mukden Incident in Yan'an". Among them, Xiao Jun and Xiao Hong emerged as the most influential representative writers. Considering these aspects as a whole, their literary contributions can be regarded as an integral and indispensable component of the history of modern Chinese literature in the 1930s.

On the other hand, due to the nature of their exilic writing, the structural composition of this group exhibited a high degree of fluidity, and their overall artistic style remained somewhat unstable. As they entered the 1940s, these writers swiftly shifted their focus to other themes, gradually losing the distinct characteristics that had once defined them, making their existence relatively short-lived. Considering these shortcomings, it becomes evident that this literary school, in many respects, remained an incomplete and less-than-perfect one.

III. Research on the "Northeastern Writers in Exile"

Understanding the history of research on the "Northeastern Writers in Exile" is of great significance in deepening our comprehension of this literary group.

With the rise of the "Northeastern Writers in Exile," scholarly inquiry into this group emerged as early as the 1930s. However, at that time, such research remained relatively scattered and lacked systematic organization. Many renowned writers and scholars of the period, such as Lu Xun, Mao Dun, Zhou Yang, Hu Qiaomu, Feng Xuefeng, Zhou Libo, and Hu Feng, all authored articles specifically analyzing and critiquing the works of Northeastern writers. It was these figures who first took notice of the emergence of "Northeastern Writers" and pioneered the academic exploration of the "Northeastern Writers in Exile." Among them, Lu Xun and Mao Dun are particularly noteworthy and deserve special mention.

What is most widely known is, first and foremost, Lu Xun's evaluation of the works of Xiao Jun and Xiao Hong, as well as his introduction of them to the cultural circles of Shanghai. Lu Xun wrote the prefaces for *Village in August* and *The Field of Life and Death*, in which he was the first to highlight the significance of *Village in August* as a work that "reveals both a part and the whole of China, the present and the future, the path to destruction and the path to survival." Regarding *The Field of Life and Death*, he praised its artistic qualities as being "so powerful that they penetrate the paper" and described its style as "brilliant and fresh." Lu Xun's critique was not only fair and insightful but also demonstrated a far-reaching vision and remarkable foresight. He grasped the very essence of these two works, capturing the historical direction they represented and illuminating their profound spiritual value—something that, at the time, had yet to be widely recognized. It is precisely through this that we can perceive Lu Xun's greatness and genius. Undoubtedly, these two prefaces will continue to be passed down alongside the books themselves.

Mao Dun's passionate praise for the creative works of Northeastern writers was often accompanied by insightful and well-balanced critiques. Although he rarely wrote prefaces for others, when he traveled to Hong Kong in 1946, apart from mourning the recent passing of his daughter, he could not help but express his deep sorrow for "Xiao Hong, who lay there in eternal rest," and thus composed a profoundly emotional eulogy, *Preface to Tales of Hulan River*.

In this piece, Mao Dun wrote: "Amidst the chaos and busyness, I managed to suppress my nostalgic feelings, yet the idea of revisiting old memories before finally letting them fade away never truly left my mind. I planned to visit Prince Edward Road in Kowloon, where I had first lived when I arrived in Hong Kong, to see the house I once stayed in, to gaze upon Butterfly Valley, where my little girl used to love inviting her friends to play... But above all, what I longed to see the most was Xiao Hong's grave—there in Repulse Bay."

Mao Dun praised *Tales of Hulan River* as "a narrative poem, a vivid and colorful landscape painting, a string of sorrowful yet beautiful folk songs." With remarkable depth, he dissected the profound "loneliness" that haunted Xiao Hong's inner world. His affection for Xiao Hong was akin to that of a father toward his daughter, and he lamented the untimely passing of this exceptionally talented female writer. In the author's view, among the numerous studies on Xiao Hong, this piece stands out as the most emotionally resonant and the most perceptive in its exploration of the depths of Xiao Hong's inner world.

Following this, several significant articles on Northeastern writers emerged in the 1930s, including Mao Dun's *Review of "Assault"*, *Tai'erzhuang*, and *Anti-Japanese Literature After the Mukden Incident: "Wanbaoshan"*, as well as Hu Qiaomu's *Review of "Village in August"*, Hu Feng's *The Breath of the Living* and *Postscript to "The Field of Life and Death"*, Luo Binji's *A Brief Biography of Xiao Hong*, Yang Sao's *Overflowing Emotions* and *The Cry of History*, Mu Mutian's *Poetry Recitation and Two Experimental Works by Mr. Gao Lan*, Mei Yu's *Monthly Review of Creative Works*, Gang Ji's *Recent Activities of Northeastern Writers*, and Ji Lyu's *Review of "Before and After the Coronation"*. Additionally, works such as Lu Xun's *The Concession in March*, Zhou Yang's *On National Defense Literature* and *TLiterature at the Present*, as well as Zhou Libo's *A Retrospective on Novel Writing in 1936—A Year of Abundance*, all contained evaluations of Northeastern writers. These articles keenly recognized the shockwaves that Northeastern writers brought to the literary scene and acknowledged the powerful role their new subject matter played in awakening the Chinese people's awareness of resistance against Japan. With great enthusiasm, they affirmed and welcomed this literary trend. By capturing the profound historical significance of the works produced by the "Northeastern Writers in Exile," these early studies ensured that research on them took the correct direction from the very beginning. The positive influence of these writings has persisted to this day, continuing to shape discussions on this important literary group.

The question of when and where the term "Northeastern Writers in Exile" first originated, while open to detailed scholarly investigation, does not appear to hold significant intrinsic importance, for the objective existence of this group and their literary achievements have long been unmistakably evident. As far as the author is aware, the concept of the "Northeastern Writers in Exile" was first introduced in 1946 in *A History of Chinese Anti-Japanese War Literature* by Lan Hai (Tian Zhongji). Later, in 1951, Wang Yao devoted an entire section to this literary group in Chapter 8 of the second volume of *A Draft History of Modern Chinese Literature*, titled *The Northeastern Writers Group*. After conducting a detailed analysis and introduction of works such as Xiao Jun's *Village in August*, Xiao Hong's *The Field of Life and Death*, as well as the literary creations of Duanmu Hongliang, Shu Qun, Luo Feng, and Bai Lang, Wang Yao concluded with the following statement:

"These works evoke a sense of anger and melancholy, playing a significant role in the awakening of national consciousness on the eve of the War of Resistance."

......

"Although these works may not yet demonstrate complete technical maturity, they serve as firsthand records of the profound suffering of a nation in peril... In fostering the awakening of national consciousness, they have undoubtedly played an inspiring role."

In addition, the history of modern Chinese literature written by Ding Yi and Liu Shaosong also mentions this literary phenomenon. Furthermore, Mr. Li Helin, in the first section of Chapter 3 of *New Literature in the Decade Around the Founding of the Association of Chinese Left-Wing Writers* (published in *Xin Jianshe Journal* in 1951), also states: "After the Mukden Incident, a group of writers from Northeast China emerged, including Xiao Jun, Xiao Hong, Shu Qun, Luo Feng, Duanmu Hongliang, Li Huiying, He Ding, and others."

Subsequently, in the keynote reports delivered at the Second and Third National Literature and Art Congress, Zhou Yang explicitly mentioned the "rise of Northeastern writers." In this way, the term "Northeastern Writers in Exile" gradually gained acceptance among scholars and the literary community, eventually becoming an established concept used to collectively refer to this group of progressive writers who emerged in the 1930s.

During the 1950s, however, several influential Northeastern writers suffered misfortunes, and for various regrettable reasons, research on modern Northeastern literature fell into a period of stagnation and silence. This prolonged state of dormancy persisted until the Third Plenary Session of the 11th Central Committee of the Communist Party, after which studies on modern Northeastern literature experienced a revival, and the term "Northeastern Writers in Exile" reemerged in academic discussions. The resurgence of research in this field attracted significant attention from scholars across China, particularly in the three Northeastern provinces, where it led the academic discourse. Writers such as Xiao Hong and Xiao Jun became widely recognized by people throughout the country, and research on the "Northeastern Writers in Exile" entered a new stage of comprehensive and systematic development.

After 1949, although research on the subject was temporarily interrupted in mainland China, studies related to the "Northeastern Writers in Exile" continued to thrive in Hong Kong and overseas regions. Scholars actively collected materials, authored books and essays, and contributed to the growing academic momentum. Li Huiying, himself a veteran writer from Northeast China, moved to Hong Kong in 1950, where he compiled *A History of Modern Chinese Literature*. In the third section of Chapter Eight, titled *Northeastern Writers in Exile*, he provided detailed introductions to nine writers, including Xiao Jun, Xiao Hong, Shu Qun, Duanmu Hongliang, Luo Binji, Bai Xiaoguang (Ma Jia), Gao Lan, and Li Huiying. Similarly, Sima Changfeng's *The History of New Chinese Literature* also examined the works of Xiao Hong, Xiao Jun, and Duanmu Hongliang, significantly contributing to the dissemination of Northeastern writers' influence within the Hong Kong literary scene. Additionally, other notable works include Zhao Fengxiang's *Xiao Hong and American Writers*, Howard Goldblatt's *Supplement to Xiao Hong and*

American Writers and *A Critical Biography of Xiao Hong*, as well as articles by Chinese-American writer Zhao Shuxia. Furthermore, Japanese scholars have produced a substantial number of academic essays on the subject. Through these domestic and international perspectives, it becomes evident that the influence of the "Northeastern Writers in Exile" has long since extended beyond China's borders, transforming into a shared cultural heritage of the global literary community. Increasingly, this body of literature is evolving into a bridge for Sino-Western cultural exchange. As a medium through which foreigners gain insight into China's history and culture, it is manifesting new historical significance.

The study of the "Northeastern Writers in Exile" has gone through a gradual process of development and refinement, during which its underlying patterns have been progressively understood. Nevertheless, this research remains incomplete and is far from reaching its final conclusion.

I believe that it is necessary to study the "Northeastern Writers in Exile" from both a systematic and comparative perspective. Each of these writers possesses distinct individual characteristics: some are bold and vigorous, while others are reserved and delicate; some are gentle and sincere, while others are simple and stubborn; some exhibit humor, some elegance, some passion, and others solemnity. Every writer and every work, while being a unique and relatively complete aesthetic entity with its own individuality, also exists within a broader system of shared aesthetic commonality, forming a collective structure. By placing a specific writer within this collective system and analyzing his particular position and value within it, we can, through comparative research with other similar writers, strive to identify the unique aesthetic attributes that belong exclusively to him. Similarly, a writer's series of works constitutes his own individual sub-system, within which each individual work occupies a distinct position. Looking at an even broader scale, the "Northeastern Writers in Exile" themselves form a sub-system within the larger system of Northeastern modern literature, while Northeastern modern literature, in turn, functions as a sub-system within the overarching system of Chinese modern literature... Such a perspective may, perhaps, allow us to broaden our horizons.

The openness and multidimensionality of perspective, the division of labor and hierarchical structure in group research, the changing angles of readers' appreciation, and the latest developments in international studies all deserve attention and should be further strengthened. We should also examine Northeastern literature within the broader context of world literature, develop a deeper understanding of the "Northeastern Writers' Group," and introduce them to the global literary stage.

Chapter 5 Xiao Hong: The Eternal Melancholic Smile

Biography

Xiao Hong (1911–1942), whose original name was Zhang Naiying and who once used the pen name Qiaoyin, was born on June 1, 1911 (the fifth day of the fifth lunar month) into a landlord family in Hulan County, Heilongjiang Province. She lost her mother at an early age and, at the age of ten, began her education at Nanguan Primary School in the county town. In 1927, at the age of sixteen, she graduated from Nanguan Primary School and was admitted to the First Girls' Middle School of the Eastern Provincial Special District in Harbin, where she was placed in Class 4 of Junior Section.

In November 1929, two anti-Japanese patriotic student movements broke out in Harbin, and Xiao Hong participated in the class boycott and the large anti-Japanese march with her classmates. During her time in middle school, Xiao Hong developed an interest in both art and literature, who joined a "Drawing Group" organized by her classmates, and one of her paintings, *Gifts from the Working People*, was well-received at the graduation ceremony's "Art Exhibition."

In July 1930, Xiao Hong received her graduation certificate from the First Girls' Middle School of the Eastern Provincial Special District and returned to Hulan. At that time, her father arranged a marriage for her with a person with the surname Wang, a frivolous and dissolute young man from Harbin. In defiance of this arranged marriage, Xiao Hong resolutely fled her family and traveled alone to Harbin, beginning a life of wandering. Shortly afterward, she went to Beiping and enrolled in the Affiliated Girls' Middle School of the Women's Normal College at Beiping University.

In 1931, Xiao Hong's "fiancé," Mr. Wang, followed her to Beijing, where he began to harass and deceive her. The two of them then returned to Harbin and stayed at the Dongxingshun Hotel. After accumulating a debt of over CNY

600, Mr. Wang made an excuse to flee, leaving the pregnant Xiao Hong behind as a hostage at the hotel.

Enduring both mental and physical torment, deceived and humiliated, Xiao Hong found herself trapped in the Dongxingshun Hotel with no way out. In the summer of 1932, in a state of despair, she wrote a letter to the *International Cooperation Daily* in Harbin, pleading for help. Eventually, she received assistance from Shu Qun, Xiao Jun, and others, and managed to escape the hotel with the help of the flooding of the Songhua River. That same autumn, Xiao Hong gave birth to a baby girl at the Harbin Municipal First Hospital. However, unable to pay for medical expenses, she had no choice but to leave the child behind at the hospital. After being discharged, she moved in with Xiao Jun, living a life of poverty and dependence. They first stayed at the Europa Hotel, and during the winter, they relocated to No. 25, Daoli Commercial Street in Harbin.

Encouraged by her close associates, including Luo Feng, Bai Lang, Shu Qun, and Jin Jianxiao, Xiao Hong began to try her hand at writing. Her first work, *The Death of Sister-in-law Wang* (published under the pen name Qiao Yin), was published in the May 1933 issue of Datong Daily in Changchun. In October of 1933, she co-authored a short story collection titled Trek with Xiao Jun, which was subsequently published.

In the summer of 1934, Xiao Hong and Xiao Jun fled from Harbin to Qingdao via Dalian. During their stay in Qingdao, she completed her novel *The Field of Life and Death*. In October, they moved to Shanghai, where she soon met Lu Xun, who recognized her talent and offered support. That same year, Xiao Hong published a collection of essays titled Commercial Street. At the end of 1935, her novel The Field of Life and Death was published as the third volume of the "Slave Series" by the Shanghai Rongguang Bookstore, which became one of the earliest literary works to reflect the lives and struggles of the people in Northeast China under Japanese imperialist rule. Lu Xun wrote the preface to the novel, praising it by saying, "The Northern people's resilience in life and their struggle with death often penetrate the pages; the female author's detailed observations and unconventional style add a lot of brightness and freshness." The publication of *The Field of Life and Death* caused a sensation in the literary world, and from then on, Xiao Hong became one of the most well-known female writers of the 1930s.

In the summer of 1936, due to health issues and growing emotional strain in her relationship with Xiao Jun, Xiao Hong traveled to Japan to recuperate. During her time in Tokyo, she wrote essays such as *Lonely Life* and *People Beyond the Family*, as well as the novel *On the Ox Cart*. In the spring of 1937, she returned to Shanghai from Tokyo, but soon traveled north to Beijing for a brief stay before heading back to Shanghai. During this period, her essay and short story collections *Bridge* and *On the Ox Cart* were successively published by the Shanghai Cultural Life Press.

After the July 7th Incident, Xiao Hong, along with people from the cultural circles of Shanghai, retreated to Wuhan, where she co-founded the magazine *July* with Hu Feng, Nie Ganmu, Xiao Jun, and others. In January 1938, at the invitation of Li Gongpu, she went to teach at the National Revolutionary University in Linfen, Shanxi. In February, she separated from Xiao Jun and went to Xi'an. In the summer, she officially divorced Xiao Jun in Xi'an and married Duanmu Hongliang, then moved south to Wuhan. In the spring of 1939, she lived with Duanmu Hongliang in Chongqing, where she wrote the short story *The Call of the Wilderness* and the essay *In Memory of Lu Xun*. During this time, she also began writing the first part of *Tales of Hulan River* in Beibei, Chongqing.

In the spring of 1940, she went to Hong Kong with Duanmu Hongliang. In December, she completed her long novel *Tales of Hulan River*. Afterward, while ill, she wrote the satirical novel Ma Bole, which analyzed the pathology of the nation and the weakness of intellectuals, and also wrote the pantomime *The National Soul, Lu Xun*. In 1941, she wrote the famous novel *March in a Small Town*, and published *The Essays of Xiao Hong* along with several short stories.

In December 1941, with the outbreak of the Pacific War and the Japanese army occupying Hong Kong, Xiao Hong fell severely ill and was bedridden. On January 13, 1942, she was transferred to the Hong Kong Sanatorium and Hospital in Happy Valley by friends. The doctors mistakenly diagnosed her condition as a throat tumor and performed surgery, but the wound did not heal. On the 18th, she was moved to Mary Hospital, where on the 19th, she lost her ability to speak. She wrote on paper: "I will dwell forever with the blue sky and clear water, leaving that half of *Dream of the Red Chamber* for others to write." She also wrote: "Half of my life was met with disdain and coldness... I die first, unwilling, unwilling." She passed away at 11:00 AM on the 22nd, at the age of only 31.

After her body was cremated, she was buried at the Shallow Water Bay Cemetery in Hong Kong. In 1957, her remains were reburied at the Eastern Galaxy Cemetery in Guangzhou.

Introduction to Works

In her short creative career of less than ten years, Xiao Hong wrote nearly a million words, displaying remarkable diligence and productivity. She was exceptionally talented, idealistic, and unique, making her one of the most beloved and influential female writers in China. She was also the most prominent among the "Northeastern Writers in Exile." Her tragic and lonely life, along with her untimely death, evokes deep sympathy and regret. Xiao Hong's artistic achievements are multifaceted, and she made significant contributions in the fields of short stories, novels, essays, and poetry. Her most influential works, which established her literary status and left a lasting impact, are her long novels *The Field of Life and Death and Tales of Hulan River*.

The Field of Life and Death was published in 1935 and immediately shook the literary world upon its release, which depicts the tragic lives and fates of the farmers in the remote Sanjiazai Village near Harbin after the Mukden Incident. The book is divided into two parts: the first ten chapters highlight the tragic lives of the farmers, emphasizing class contradictions, while the latter seven chapters focus on national conflicts, addressing the urgent issue of the status and future of Northeast farmers after the Mukden Incident.

What leaves the deepest impression in the novel is the suffering endured by the Northeast farmers, who lead a life that is nearly primitive and slave-like, seemingly unable to escape the control of fate. For instance, the peasant woman, Wang Po, sells her old horse to pay off debts, yet receives only "the price of a horsehide," while "the landlord's agents are already waiting at the door, as landlords never spare even a single copper coin from the poor farmers," and this small amount of money is also taken away. The author indignantly writes, "Wang Po's half-day of suffering has no price! All her life's suffering is without value." Moreover, a month-old infant, the daughter of Jin Zhi, is cruelly thrown to her death by her father, who views her as a burden preventing him from paying off his debts. At the same time, Fifth Aunt's sister gives birth naked, writhing like a fish on a clay stove, enduring abuse from her husband until she "lies in a pool of blood, her body drenched in blood," with the child also "dying in birth." In the background, "behind the house, on a grass heap, the dogs are giving birth," which serves as a symbolic contrast between humans and animals. This stark and authentic portrayal of the suffering of Northeast farmers reflects their spiritual bondage to feudalism, brutal economic oppression by landlords, and a tragic existence that places them in a status no better than that of pigs or dogs. The writer, with a detached yet steady hand, deeply explores the fate of these farmers while expressing profound sympathy for their suffering.

In the second part of the novel, the author shifts focus and highlights the more direct and sharp root cause of the Northeast farmers' tragic fate — the invasion of Japanese imperialism. The work states, "The banner of 'benevolent rule' came, and everywhere there was arson, killing, and plundering. All the young women in the village fled, and even thirteen-year-old girls were not spared by the Japanese soldiers!" The farmland lay desolate, and the number of widows increased. Wang Po even yearns for the past, for "today's days are worse than yesterday's." When the farmers, at last, demonstrated "an iron-like will to fight" on this "blurry land soaked with blood" (as noted by Hu Feng in the *Postscript to "The Field of Life and Death"*), and when they collectively pledged to resist the Japanese, even the widows, shedding tears, knelt down with "the gun aimed at their hearts" to take the oath, and when the former "kind-hearted" Zhao San shouted, "Even if I'm buried in a grave... I'll plant the Chinese flag on top of my grave. I am Chinese!" When such words echoed and the cries of the people "drove into each person's chest like a wedge, and when a strong wave of sorrow swept through the lowered heads, the vast blue sky seemed on the verge of collapsing," a powerful scene of the Northeast farmers' oath to resist unfolded before the reader. The once "ant-like ignorant men and women" now stood bravely on the frontlines of a sacred national war, no longer "ant-like living for death," but rather, "giant-like living for life" (as described by Hu Feng in the *Postscript to "The Field of Life and Death"*). Before the enemy's bayonets, they had finally awakened — the ants had transformed into giants, which was a great awakening and elevation, representing the historical will of the Chinese nation. As Mr. Lu Xun said, "It shows a part and the whole of China, the present and the future, the dead end and the road to survival." The resolute national integrity is where the novel profoundly conveys the aesthetic significance of the era.

The Field of Life and Death also places significant emphasis on the portrayal of the character of Northeast farmers, particularly in depicting their inner spirit. Xiao Hong pays special attention to the deep emotional connection that Northeast farmers have with their land and livestock. She describes the details of Wang Po, who is forced to sell her horse to pay off debts; Zhao San, who is compelled to sell his cow; and Er Li Ban, who finds it difficult to part with his beloved old goat despite joining the anti-Japanese forces. These moments reflect the normal mentality of farmers living under the feudal and self-sustaining agricultural economy of Northeast China, which is shaped by their economic status and dependence on small-scale farming. Xiao Hong's artistic sensitivity and keen observational skills are truly remarkable.

The Field of Life and Death does have some shortcomings, such as a somewhat disorganized structure and occasionally awkward language. However, these flaws are overshadowed by the work's dazzling ideas and artistic charm, where the imperfections do not detract from its brilliance. In fact, some of the awkward sentences, which clearly reveal the author's own literary limitations, are even accepted as part of the author's unique style. Although somewhat immature, the writing is sincere and therefore deeply moving, which is a characteristic common to many Northeast writers.

Tales of Hulan River, another masterpiece by Xiao Hong, not only allows readers to fully understand her and her unique style but also highlights her artistic talent and distinctive approach to novel writing.

Tales of Hulan River, a novel with a distinct style, is also a beautiful piece of prose, beginning with a portrayal of the relationship between man and nature, vividly sketching the unique, colorful customs of the northern town of Hulan, where the harsh winter, the spirit-calling rituals, yangko dances, river lantern festivals, folk theater, and the annual temple fair come to life, creating the distinctive sounds and atmosphere of a northern town in the 1920s. The novel further depicts the monotonous lifestyle of its people, who, year after year, endure the cold spring and autumn weather, living in petty, mundane routines where "when a person dies, it's over," and though there is beauty in the northern people's goodness, hard work, and perseverance, there is also ignorance, conservatism, and pettiness, forming a sickly national soul, representing the passive, numb adaptation of farmers living under backward productive forces. While the author's tone is calm, as if recounting distant memories of the northern past, it gradually weighs heavily on the reader's heart, leading them to reflect deeply on the backwardness of the national spirit, while also loudly denouncing the destructive influence of feudal forces on the souls of farmers.

Tales of Hulan River presents characters whose symbolic meanings are profound. Among them is the pitiful figure of the second uncle, who "looked neither like a monkey trainer nor a beggar ," living in an unfortunate situation, yet even more tragic is the numbness of his soul. He exists in a slave-like position, blindly loyal to the feudal hierarchy, believing that a slave is forever a slave, and a master is always a master, and that a slave should never "rebel against their master." With the dissection of the national soul, Xiao Hong, in a heavy mood, delves deeply into the inherent flaws and pathological lives of the northeastern Chinese peasants under the old system. The tortured fate of the younger daughter-in-law, the silent, strong, and resilient Feng Moguan, and the fate, gestures, and actions of other ordinary characters are all vividly recreated by Xiao Hong. Through the bloodstains of the feudal shackles, she sincerely calls for a vibrant and natural life. With her works, she conveys her reflections on life and society, creating a profound, weighty sense of history and thought-provoking philosophical insight, making the work endlessly memorable.

The beauty of *Tales of Hulan River* is a fusion of multiple elements, with its essay-like structural approach, subtle and restrained lyrical style, and naturally sparse yet profound artistic conception collectively shaping a distinctive formal aesthetic, while the "emotion" embedded in the work resembles a lingering and sorrowful melody that winds and echoes throughout the text, at times resonating with pure and bright notes, and at other times murmuring with melancholic and desolate undertones; it appears both as the voice of one who has endured hardships and whose heart is scarred by suffering, and as that of a childlike soul perpetually seeking solace in the longing for beauty; it embodies both a lashing critique of evil and a mournful outcry against death, yet simultaneously sings praises of life and expresses a fervent yearning for beauty; the silent sorrow and the tear-stained laughter, interwoven seamlessly, construct the complex inner emotions of Xiao Hong, and this very "emotion," infused with her reflections on the journey of life and her deep-seated concern for the fate of her homeland, flows like a gentle stream, permeating the reader's heart and carrying an irresistible artistic power.

Xiao Hong's short stories are also remarkably well-written. Although her early works, such as *The Death of Sister-in-law Wang*, *The Assistant Advertiser*, *Watching the Kite*, and *Night Wind*, written in Harbin, still exhibited a somewhat immature style, revealing her budding literary talent. Deeply familiar with the lives of Northeast farmers, she used a somewhat heavy-handed narrative style to depict the suffering of the people under the rule of the Japanese puppet regime. From the very beginning of her literary career, her works carried a distinct progressive political inclination, and the somber and poignant tone of her writing remained unchanged throughout her career. In *The Death of Sister-in-law Wang*, the tragic demise of the protagonist, in *The Assistant Advertiser*, the struggles of urban intellectuals in Northeast China as they desperately seek to make a living, and in *Night Wind*, the depiction of a peasant uprising, all serve as powerful portrayals that capture the defining characteristics and spirit of the people in that era. After fleeing to the south of the Great Wall, Xiao Hong produced several outstanding short stories, including *People Beyond the Family*, *On the Ox Cart, Hands*, and *March in a Small Town. People Beyond the Family* reflects her childhood experiences, centering on her second uncle, whose sorrowful life and sincere emotions can be seen as a precursor to a character later developed in *Tales of Hulan River. On the Ox Cart* tells the tragic story of Wu Yunsao, a rural woman whose desperate pleas to her husband and ultimate disillusionment mirror Xiao Hong's own silent lament over her fate. The novel was written around the time she traveled to Japan, further revealing her profound contemplation on the hardships of life and society. Hands demonstrates a further refinement of Xiao Hong's artistic techniques, with the female student Wang Yaming's inner turmoil and the oppressive forces of society leaving a lasting impression on readers. Meanwhile, *March in a Small Town* surpasses her earlier works in both artistic individuality and technical execution. However, one slight drawback is that the emotions within the story are conveyed with an excessively melancholic tone, and the narrative style seems almost overly sentimental.

Xiao Hong's poetry is also remarkable. Her earliest works, written during her time in Harbin, are deeply genuine:

"Here, the leaves grow fresh and bright,
There, the brook sings with delight:
— Oh, fair maiden!
Spring is here...

Last year's May,
I tasted green apricots in old Beijing's way.
This year's May,
My life is filled with pain,
As bitter as those fruits again!

With a simple and unembellished tone, Xiao Hong expressed her sighs over her own fate, her resentment toward a dark reality, and her longing for a brighter future, evoking deep sympathy for the talented yet struggling young woman. Her poetry collection *Sand Grains*, written during her time in Tokyo, attracted much attention for its scattered, melancholic verses, which share a similar emotional tone with *The Bitter Cup*, conveying both the anguish of emotional torment and a condemnation of love's betrayal. Filled with raw intensity and sorrowful restraint, these poems vividly reflect Xiao Hong's distressing state of mind around 1936. Varying in form but primarily focused on expressing personal sentiments, her poetry also includes other notable works such as *Tomb Tribute and A Clod of Earth*.

A Beauty That Dazzles and Bewilders

Xiao Hong's friend, Luo Binji, once spoke of her, saying: "Surrounded by the forces of a semi-feudal, semi-colonial society, Xiao Hong, as a mere twenty-year-old girl, managed to carve out a path for herself; without extraordinary resilience, unyielding defiance, and immense courage, she would have long since been led down a road to destruction." As a warrior challenging a dark society, she was remarkable; as a writer with a distinct artistic identity, she was successful; and as a woman of deep emotions, her heart always beat for the people. Born amid the ice and snow of the North, yet resting eternally beneath the kapok trees of the South, her life of hardship and wandering evokes profound sympathy and sorrow. Both her character and her literary works continue to command admiration and awe.

Xiao Hong was a writer with a distinctive artistic style, but how can one truly grasp and understand the essence of her artistry?

Her works possess a unique beauty, which Mao Dun once praised, saying that *Tales of Hulan River* was "so beautiful it dazzles and bewilders." This beauty lies in the natural and fluid quality of her prose, where the softness of form seamlessly blends with the strength of its inner spirit. Xiao Hong's aesthetic ideals manifest through her highly individualistic creations, generating a profound artistic effect. The essence of her unique aesthetic approach can be summarized in the following key points:

1. The Creation of Tragic Beauty

Xiao Hong was a master of crafting tragic beauty, and the inescapable fates of her characters have moved countless readers. She excelled in depicting the tragedies of ordinary people, particularly those of Northeastern farmers and young women: characters like Yueying, Aunt Cui, Younger Daughter-in-law, Wang Po, Jinzhi, Her Second Uncle, and Feng Moguan, who moan in suffering, struggle on the edge of life and death, as if crying out: "Save me!" Xiao Hong deeply explored the historical and societal forces that led to their misery, paying special attention to the immense devastation the Mukden Incident brought upon the people of Northeast China. By situating individual tragedies within a broader historical context, she revealed their profound aesthetic significance. Through her works, readers not only witness the suffering of her characters but also gain insight into a tragic historical era, appreciating the depth of the tragic effect embedded in her artistry.

2. The Allure of Nostalgic Beauty

Xiao Hong had a remarkable talent for selecting material, particularly drawing inspiration from her early life, which she knew intimately. In both her fiction and essays, she often found herself unconsciously immersed in memories of the past. This deep sense of recollection became a defining feature of her work. She reminisced about her childhood with great affection, recalling the customs of her hometown in Hulan, the vast, snow-covered fields of winter, and the everyday lives of Northeastern farmers. As her life journey unfolded, these memories grew stronger and more profound, blending with the hardships of her exile and the fresh wounds of new sorrows, elevating her emotions to a state of greater depth, sincerity, and purity. Seeping into her writing, these refined emotions silently resonate with the reader, fostering a deep emotional connection. As Mao Dun described, her work becomes "a narrative poem, a vibrant landscape of local customs, and a sorrowful ballad strung together in verse." (*Preface to Tales of Hulan River*, Mao Dun)

3. The Creation of Artistic Ambience

Xiao Hong's works often present a blend of both haziness and clarity, where the pure beauty of nature intertwines with a somber emotional atmosphere, and the external realities of life coexist with profound philosophical reflection. Combining elements of poetry, prose, and painting, her writing integrates sound, light, and color into a single artistic experience like a gentle breeze sweeping across the vast northern wilderness, evoking both a sense of freshness and a lingering heaviness. This unique style creates an ethereal yet profound artistic ambience, deeply infused with her emotional undertones. The deeper and more natural the artistic realm, the more intense the emotions it conveys, enhancing its aesthetic value. This characteristic, so reflective of Xiao Hong's artistic temperament and deeply tied to the realities of life, is particularly evident in *Tales of Hulan River*.

4. **The Poignant Beauty of Solitude**

Xiao Hong's life, as reflected in her works, seems to be filled with few moments of joy, with loneliness and hardship accompanying her to the very end. In her later years in Hong Kong, she lived in seclusion, and her writings took on an increasingly melancholic tone, mirroring her solitude.

Yet, what is truly remarkable is how this sorrowful loneliness unexpectedly transforms into a unique aesthetic experience within her works. Rather than succumbing to despair, Xiao Hong sought to submerge her solitude in the act of creation. Out of this lonely state of mind emerged some of her finest works such as *Tales of Hulan River*, *March in a Small Town*, and *Ma Bole*, achieving new artistic heights. She wove her personal sorrow and isolation into a profound love for her homeland, ultimately transcending solitude through her art. Her contemplative soul radiated a passionate ode to life and human existence, and even in her final moments, she continued to fight with unyielding determination. The "tiny flickering light" within her never dimmed, always shining toward her country and her people. At the peak of her emotional suffering, her works still carried the spirit of the times. The solitude expressed in her later writings transcended mere personal loneliness and ascended into the realm of artistic creation, giving birth to a new aesthetic—the beauty of solitude, which was a beauty rooted in defiance, in an unrelenting struggle against fate. Like a phoenix reborn from fire, the "solitary Xiao Hong" remains eternally alive in the hearts of those who remember her!

Chapter 6 Xiao Jun: The Struggle of the Oppressed

Biography

Xiao Jun (1907–1988), originally named Liu Honglin, and also known by the pen names San Lang, Tian Jun, and Liu Jun, was born on the 23rd day of the 5th month in the lunar calendar, 1907, in Xiayan Pangou Village, Shenjiatai Town, Yixian County, Liaoning (now part of Jinzhou City, Liaoning Province). His grandfather, Liu Rong, was a tenant farmer, and his father was Liu Qinglian.

At the age of six, Xiao Jun began studying in a local private school. At eighteen, in order to make a living, he joined a cavalry camp in Jilin City as a cavalryman, where he started reading progressive literary works. In 1928, he was admitted to the 9th and 10th classes of the Northeast Army Military Academy's artillery department. Not long after, he published his first novel, *Coward...* in the *Shengjing Times*, which depicted the life of soldiers under warlord rule. In the spring of 1930, he was expelled from the academy for advocating justice, and he later worked as a lieutenant in the Northeast Army Military Police Training Department, teaching military and martial arts. After the Mukden Incident in 1931, Xiao Jun went to Shulan County in Jilin, where he secretly organized an anti-Japanese volunteer army with friends. The army was defeated, and Xiao Jun moved to Harbin, where he officially began his literary career under the pen name "San Lang."

In 1932, he met Xiao Hong, and they began living together. In 1933, they jointly published a short story collection titled Trek.

In August 1934, due to economic and political pressures, Xiao Jun left Harbin with Xiao Hong, traveling via Dalian to Qingdao for a brief stay. In November, they arrived in Shanghai, where they met Lu Xun and became involved in editorial work for the magazines *The Petrel* and *Writers*, engaging in left-wing literary activities. In July 1935, his novel *Village in August* was published, with a preface by Lu Xun, who highly praised it. The novel was widely appreciated by progressive readers, and from that point on, Xiao Jun gained widespread recognition in the literary world.

In October 1936, Xiao Jun participated in the funeral arrangements for the late Lu Xun, serving as the chief commander of the funeral procession and also contributing to the editing of the *Memorial Collection of Lu Xun*.

After the outbreak of the Shanghai Anti-Japanese War in 1937, Xiao Jun and Xiao Hong left Shanghai for Wuhan, where they, along with Hu Feng and others, co-edited the magazine *July*. In early 1938, Xiao Jun was invited to teach at the Shanxi National Revolution University in Linfen. In March of the same year, he walked to Yan'an and later joined the "Northwest Battlefield Service Groups." After arriving in Xi'an with Ding Ling, Xiao Jun officially separated from Xiao Hong. Although he initially planned to go to Xinjiang, he did not go and instead traveled to Lanzhou, where he met Wang Defen and got married. Together with Wang, he moved to Chengdu via Xi'an, where he worked as an editor at the *Xinmin Daily*.

In the summer of 1940, Xiao Jun made a second trip to Yan'an. He held several positions, including director of the Chinese Association of Literary and Art Circles for Resisting Enemy, director of the Lu Xun Research Society in Yan'an, editor for *Literature Monthly*, and a lecturer in the "Lu Xun's Art" literature department. He also participated in the Yan'an Literary and Art Symposium.

In 1945, Xiao Jun traveled to Zhangjiakou with the literary troupe. In the autumn of 1946, he arrived in Harbin. In November, he went to Jiamusi, where he became the dean of the Lu Xun Arts and Literature College at Northeast University. In the spring of 1947, he returned to Harbin, where he served as the president of the Lu Xun Cultural Publishing House and the editor-in-chief of *Literary News*. He later faced unjust criticism. In 1949, Xiao Jun went to work at the Fushun Mining Bureau, where he experienced the life of coal miners, which laid the foundation for his novel *The Mines of May*.

In 1951, Xiao Jun moved to Beijing, where he worked as a researcher for the Beijing Cultural Relics Group and as a researcher for the Beijing Peking Opera Directing Committee, while also continuing his literary creation. During the "Cultural Revolution", he was once again persecuted, and it wasn't until the downfall of the "Gang of Four" that he made a comeback. In 1979, he participated in the 4th National Literature and Arts Congress, where he was elected as a member of the National Federation of Literary and Art Circles and a council member of the Chinese Writers' Association. In 1980, the Beijing Municipal Committee of the Communist Party of China made an official political assessment of Xiao Jun, affirming that he was "a revolutionary writer who supports the Communist Party of China, supports socialism, and has national integrity."

After his return to public life, Xiao Jun traveled to the United States and Singapore for academic exchanges and also gave lectures in various parts of China. His novel Village in August was reissued. Throughout his life, he pursued the goal of establishing a system of social justice where the independence of the country, the liberation of the nation, and the empowerment of the people were realized, and where no one exploited or oppressed others. He dedicated his life to the people, earning their love and respect.

Xiao Jun passed away in Beijing in 1988 at the age of 81.

Introduction to Works

Xiao Jun's most famous novel is *Village in August.*

Alongside Xiao Hong's *The Field of Life and Death*, it stood as one of the most representative works of the Chinese left-wing literary scene in the early 1930s, becoming a prominent example among the "Northeastern Writers in Exile."

Village in August tells the story of a Chinese anti-Japanese guerrilla force that bravely fights against the enemy following the Mukden Incident. The novel authentically portrays the courageous resistance of the people in Northeast China. The guerrilla force in the novel is subtly hinted to be under the leadership of the Chinese Communist Party. Despite facing hunger, fatigue, and enemy resistance, the soldiers' morale remains high. They support one another, singing the *International Anthem*, and march forward through the storm of battle. This serves as a vivid reflection of the rising anti-Japanese forces in Northeast China following the Mukden Incident. Although the group is small, like a trickling stream, such small streams will eventually merge into a vast river of national resistance against Japan. Lu Xun once said, "Art and literature are the sparks of a nation's spirit, and at the same time, they are the guiding light for the nation's future." *Village in August* powerfully expressed the call for national salvation through resistance against Japan. By focusing on this small guerrilla force, the novel vividly captured the theme of the era, and at a time when the nation was suffering under deepening national calamity, the book allowed the people to breathe a sigh of relief.

In 1934, as the White Terror intensified in Shanghai, the Left-wing Writers' Alliance also faced severe suppression. It was at this critical moment that *Village in August* emerged, which boldly portrayed the brutal reality of Northeast China under Japanese occupation. It loudly called for the advent of anti-Japanese literature and represented a new direction in literary creation, with significant practical implications. Lu Xun, not only out of personal affection but also recognizing the urgent need for such works at the time, praised the novel. In his preface, he wrote: "I have seen several novels about the occupation of the Three Eastern Provinces. *Village in August* is one of the best. … The author's efforts and the lost skies, lands, suffering people, and even the lost tall grasses, sorghum, crickets, and mosquitoes all come together in a vivid, bloody scene that unfolds before the reader's eyes, displaying a piece of China in the present and future, both its dead ends and its paths to survival." Qiao Mu remarked that the novel "brought a whole new scene to the Chinese literary world. A new theme, new characters, and new background." From that moment, the suffering and struggles of the people in Northeast China lived on in the emotions and lives of the entire nation.

The characters in the novel are vivid and dynamic. The guerrilla leader, Tie Ying, is a tough, strong-willed man with a deep, tender affection for his comrades, making him a very moving and compelling figure as a commander. Xiao Ming and Anna, the intellectuals in the revolutionary team, are brave and resolute, working actively in the struggle. However, due to the conflict between love and revolution, they experience moments of weakness in their character. The author keenly observes the specific characteristics of intellectuals participating in the revolution: they are full of enthusiasm but also have ideological weaknesses, which highlights the necessity for intellectuals to connect with the working-class masses and grow through actual struggle. Xiao Jun was one of the first to clearly capture the era's choice for intellectuals to walk the path of revolution. Another moving figure is Li Qisha, a young peasant woman. After the enemy kills her lover, violates her body, and kills her child, she struggles to stand up, picks up her lover's gun, and courageously joins the ranks of the avengers. From that moment, she begins a deadly fight against the invaders, who symbolizes the awakening of the peasantry in Northeast China. In addition, there are characters like Tang Laogeda, who symbolizes the conflict between personal love and revolutionary discipline. He wants to resist the Japanese but is always hesitant, saying, "Let's talk about it in a few days... When the Japanese come, then we'll deal with it." There is also the young peasant Tian Laoba, who falls into empty revolutionary idealism, and the fearless soldier Li Sandi, among other characters, each with distinctive personalities, all portrayed with vivid and touching detail.

Village in August features a bold and powerful approach to character creation, with characters who exude masculinity and solemnity, perfectly aligning with the harsh times depicted in the novel. The work showcases a rugged beauty, capturing the essence of an era marked by struggle. Additionally, the language used in the novel is direct and forceful, with a strong sense of realism and regional flavor, which greatly enhances its artistic appeal. In many ways, the novel is influenced by Soviet literature, particularly the novel *Destruction*.

The Past Years (also known as *The Third Generation*) is another of Xiao Jun's famous novels, with the first part published in the wartime journal *July*, which is set against the broad historical backdrop of the period from the Xinhai Revolution to the eve of the Anti-Japanese War. It tells the story of the suffering and struggles of poor peasants in a mountain village along the Daling River in Western Liaoning. The structure of the novel is grand, with a large historical scope, vast settings, and a wide array of characters. The customs and local color of Western Liaoning, along with the vibrant atmosphere of the times, are distinctly portrayed. The novel took several years to complete and is regarded as a symbol of Xiao Jun's mature creative skills.

It begins in a remote mountain village and moves to the urban city of Changchun, which depicts the cruel oppression of peasants by the local "landlord" Yang Luozhong, who colludes with the officials and soldiers, and follows the peasants as they rise in rebellion, ultimately fleeing to the cities, amidst the turbulence of the times. The novel's deeper meaning lies in its exploration of the tragic fate of the Northeast peasantry, using their struggles to reflect the broader historical era. What is most striking in the novel is the exploration of the character of the Northeast peasants.

This is a strange land, a history of rise and fall. The land is both wild and rich, both dormant and ever-changing. The history is laden with the heavy remnants of feudalism and ripples with the stirring of a nation's awakening soul, pulsing in the silence. The traditional, insular feudal economic structure, the tumultuous modern history, and especially the invasion of Japanese imperialism, all contributed to the unique and complex character of the Northeast peasantry, shaped by these specific historical conditions. In the novel, characters like Jing Quanlong and Lin Qing are portrayed as farmers who dare to defy the power of the ruling class. They possess fiery, brave, and straightforward personalities, representing the rebellious spirit of the Northeast peasants. They organize and resist, driven by a strong sense of revolt, embodying the "wildness" of the Northeast. In contrast, characters like Wang Dabianzi symbolize the servitude of the peasantry. He is selfish, ignorant, cowardly, and self-deceiving, fearing both the landlords and the "bandits" constantly accepting his fate. His appearance, wearing a fox fur hat with the earflaps not fastened, looking like the wings of a crow, along with a small braid from the Qing Dynasty hanging at the back of his head, presents a pitiful and laughable image. Every action of his reflects the mentality of small peasant landowners, who passively adapt to their environment in a state of apathetic resignation, which is tragically pitiable. This portrayal is highly successful. Cuiping, fierce and bold, is the most moving female character in the novel. She represents Xiao Jun's deep understanding of the inner spiritual qualities of Northeast peasant women. Cuiping dares to join the "bandits" on her own, confronts the landlords face-to-face, and is unafraid of conflict, embodying the wildness of young Northeast women. She is a character who inspires hope, like a sharp point, though the author weakens her character's brilliance in the later parts of the novel. Other characters, like Song Qiyue, Liu Yuan, and Hai Jiao, each have their own distinct traits. Some are passionate, others silent, some unafraid of taking risks, while others repeatedly avoid conflict and isolation, reflecting the overall character of the Northeast peasantry. The peasants' complex character is a mixture of hard work, simplicity, honesty, and selfishness, with both resistance and submission coexisting, and is the character shaped by over two thousand years of feudal ideas and the pressures of real social life. What's more, it is inevitably forged in the fire of anti-Japanese resistance. However, when the storm of war first arrives, they are confused, struggling to find their way, unsure of which path to take. Xiao Jun's works pay great attention to analyzing the contradictory characteristics of the Northeast peasants shaped by their specific historical conditions. This deep understanding of the social life of Northeast China and its peasants is the result of Xiao Jun's profound insight.

After 1949, Xiao Jun faced prolonged and erroneous criticism, which significantly affected his creative work. Other major works of his include the novels *The Mines of May*, *A Historical Account of the Spring and Autumn Period of Wu and Yue*, the novella *Trickling Streams*, the play *The Happy Home*, the Peking opera *The Tragic Story of Ma Zhenhua*, the short story collections *Trek*, *Sheep*, *On the River*, the essay collections *The Story of Green Leaves* and *October 15th*, as well as some memoirs and other writings.

The Sturdy and Majestic Poplar

Amidst the vast northeastern plains, a robust species of poplar thrives, standing tall and unyielding with its thick trunk and deep-rooted foundation. Undeterred by the harshest cold, it braves the wind and snow with unwavering resilience, and when spring arrives, it bursts forth with vigorous vitality. Much like this towering poplar, Xiao Jun's literary style exudes a rugged, powerful, and uninhibited spirit. A closer analysis reveals several defining characteristics:

1. Staying Closely Aligned with Real Life and Reflecting the Grand Themes of the Era

Xiao Jun, known for his bold and outspoken nature, possessed an indomitable spirit akin to a tireless machine that never ceased its motion. His works, much like his character, always stood at the forefront of the times. With an unrestrained and forceful writing style, he vividly depicted the turbulent and stormy realities of life, ensuring that his works resonated deeply with the overarching themes of his era. Rather than indulging in frivolous and escapist tales of idle romance, he remained steadfast in his commitment to portraying the struggles of reality. As Lu Xun remarked in *Collected Letters of Lu Xun*, *Village in August* was "filled with passion, completely different from the works of so-called 'writers' who merely toy with technique," a keen observation that precisely captured this defining characteristic of Xiao Jun's writing.

In his early years in Harbin, Xiao Jun co-authored the short story collection *Trek* with Xiao Hong, drawing from his own life experiences to depict the suffering of the lower-class people in Japanese-occupied Northeast China, particularly the plight of impoverished and destitute intellectuals. The struggling young literature enthusiast in *The Crimson Thread* and *Candle's Heart*, as well as the elderly man in *This Is a Common Occurrence*, who, despite his frailty, continues chopping firewood to survive until his eventual demise, all reflect the writer's clear political stance, deep emotional convictions, and his fearless challenge to society. Xiao Jun possessed a keen ability to grasp the aesthetic trends of his time, aligning his creative works with the urgent themes of the era. Through his own experiences, he became acutely aware of the pressing necessity of the Anti-Japanese War and the national salvation movement. His writing transcended the narrow sphere of an intellectual's personal struggles, reaching into the lives of the working class, embracing society at large, and pulsating with the rhythm of the times. This ability to connect with broader social realities was a fundamental reason why his works quickly gained attention and achieved success. In his short story *Cherry Blossoms*, he portrays the experiences of patriotic intellectuals from the Northeast who migrate to the interior, highlighting the deep humiliation inflicted upon the people by the term "conquered subjects." Other stories, such as *The Sheep*, *On the River*, *Profession*, and *The Widower*, depict the immense suffering brought upon the Chinese people by Japanese aggression. However, in *Village in August*, while there is sorrow and humiliation, the dominant theme is one of resistance. What makes this work so compelling is its irrepressible spirit; as one reads, an unstoppable force seems to surge from its pages. The story moves with a wild and untamed energy, much like the ocean and flames, with its grand momentum embodying the beauty of strength. Lu Xun once praised it as a timely "spear" because it resonated with the powerful voice of the era.

2. Rugged Prose, Dynamic Plot, and Unrestrained Emotion

Xiao Jun's writing is bold, forceful, and brimming with intensity. In *Village in August*, the torrential downpour that strikes without warning, the anti-Japanese soldiers marching urgently through the muddy terrain, the flickering bonfires at their campsite, the drooping red flags, the sobbing hills, the solemn burial of fallen heroes, the neighing of warhorses, the sky weeping, and the poignant moment when Li Qisao picks up her slain lover's rifle all evoke a raw and rugged sense of beauty. In *The Past Years*, he paints a striking contrast between the eerie gloom of government prisons, the opulent estates of landlords, and the bustling streets of Changchun, interwoven with the hunger and wandering of displaced villagers, the rising smoke from the bandits' camp in Qingsha Mountain, and the restless surge of events. Xiao Jun's distinct style emerges through the shifts in time and space, the dramatic and sweeping variations in narrative intensity, and the profound emotional depth, all of which contribute to its boldness, vigor, and dynamic energy.

Xiao Jun's *Village in August* is characterized by a highly fragmented narrative, with each chapter standing independently, resembling a sequence of cinematic shots. Therefore, Lu Xun described it as "a near-continuous series of short stories." Even in its language and narration, readers may sense certain ruptures and gaps. Rather than focusing on grand, panoramic depictions, the author channels his energy into precise and vivid portrayals of smaller, individual moments, which ultimately defines his unique writing style. While this approach conveys a raw and unconventional beauty that feels bold and refreshing in its departure from tradition, it also exposes certain shortcomings, particularly in the author's limited familiarity with real-life experiences.

Xiao Jun's writing is marked by an unrestrained emotional expressiveness, with his passion laid bare on the page, pulsating like the rapid, resonant beats of a drum. This intensity gives his work a powerful sense of immediacy and emotional impact, a quality that seems closely tied to the urgency of the wartime era. Much like the rallying cry of "Arise, ye who suffer from hunger and cold," when the Chinese nation stood at the brink of survival, this kind of direct and impassioned call to action was precisely what the times demanded.

3. A Strong Regional Atmosphere

Xiao Jun once spoke with deep affection: "I grew up in northern Manchuria, and I love the boundless, snow-covered plains. I love the infinitely high blue sky, the ink-black pine and cypress forests, the towering birch trees that seem forged from silver, and the poplars standing tall and straight. I love the surging herds of cattle and sheep like foaming waves, but above all, I love the bold and forthright people... Without them, my soul feels lonely." (*The Story of Green Leaves*, Xiao Jun).

On the dark, oil-like fields, endless red sorghum sways in the wind; in the dense forests, pine branches stretch upward, reaching for the sky; amidst the grasses, crickets sing their melodies, and the intoxicating scent of the earth fills the air... These scenes, mixed with the author's deep nostalgia, exude the unique charm of the northeastern plains, which is the vibrant, bustling wilderness brought to life in Xiao Jun's *Village in August*:

"In the air, the scent of various half-ripe grains mixes and drifts constantly. Sorghum! Soybeans! … In early September, the men and women in the fields laugh as they work busily. Large carts are piled high with bundles, neatly tied. Children, barefoot beneath, still wear last winter's cotton coats, running and shouting..."

The bustling and lively fields, the rising smoke from the thatched huts, and the beauty of the northeastern land are all vivid in Xiao Jun's writing. The hunting of wild rabbits, frying fresh roe deer meat, spirit-calling rituals, ancestor worship, the sounds of shouting for pigs and ducks, and the lively scenes of wedding celebrations all embody the rich atmosphere of rural life in Northeast China, making the scenes all the more moving. As for the icy, snowy world of the northern winter, it is equally captivating. The beauty of the land and the pain of losing it intertwine, creating a powerful emotional vortex that resonates deeply with readers, the aesthetic impact being self-evident.

Xiao Jun is an exceptionally talented writer. His works not only have a grand and majestic side but also a delicate and graceful one. When his pen delves into the inner workings of characters' minds, the narrative becomes fuller and more genuine. His ability to combine roughness with meticulous detail, strength with naturalness, defines his style and leaves a lasting impression on readers.

Chapter 7 Duanmu Hongliang: The Gallop on the Horqin Grassland

Biography

Duanmu Hongliang (1912-1996), formerly known as Cao Jingping, used the pen name of Huang Ye, Luo Xuan, Ye Zhilin, Cao Ping, Jin Yongni, etc., Manchu. In September 25, 1912, he was born in a large landowner's family in Cilushu Village, Changtu County, Liaoning Province. His father had traveled to the south and was influenced by the new ideas of bourgeois democracy. Her mother was the daughter of a local tenant farmer named Huang. Since childhood, Duanmu was influenced by his mother and sympathized with the suffering of the working people.

In 1918, Duanmu Hongliang went to Changtu County Elementary School, and in 1923, he went to junior high school in Huiwen Middle School run by Americans in Tianjin. After only one year of study, because of the outbreak of the Zhili–Fengtian War, his father called him back to his hometown to self-study and practice writing and painting at home. During this period, he gained a deeper understanding of the situation in the rural areas of Northeast China and the hardship of the local farmers. In 1927, he studied in Changtu County Middle School.

In 1928, he was admitted to Tianjin Nankai Middle School for his third year of junior high school. He read widely progressive literature and came into contact with Marxist ideology, and is more and more progressive-minded, and showed his literary talent. He became the president of the Nankai Fine Arts Society and the editor of the school magazine. He and his classmates published the new publication *Human World* and *New Man* and organized the New Man Society. His debut novel, *Shuisheng*, was published in *New Man*. At about the same time, he also published *The Literary Manifesto of Force* and was actively engaged in progressive literary activities.

After the Mukden Incident, he was expelled from school for organizing progressive students to form the Anti-Japanese Salvation League. After that, he participated in the students' demonstration to the south. In the spring of 1932, he joined Sun Dianying's 41st Army. In the summer, he returned to Peking. In the fall, he was admitted to the history department of Tsinghua University. In 1932, he joined the Pecking Association of Chinese Left-Wing Writers and edited Science News, the organ magazine of the association.

At Tsinghua University, Duanmu Hongliang began to write his long novel *Horqin Banner Grassland*, and in 1933 he began to correspond with Lu Xun under the pen name Ye Zhilin. A part of the novel was published in Tsinghua University's *Weekly News*. In August 1933, the novel was finished and the first draft was sent to Mr. Zheng Zhenduo, who evaluated it as "the longest in China for more than ten years" and "excellent in quality", and indicated that he would try his best to assist in publishing it soon. But due to various reasons, it was not until 1939 that this book, which depicts the lives of the people in Northeast China on the eve of the Mukden Incident, was published by Kaiming Bookstore.

In 1935, Duanmu took part in the December 9th Movement in Peking and then went to Shanghai. In 1936, in Shanghai, he wrote a short story *Melancholy of the Cilu Lake*, which was published in *Literature* and well received. From then on, his creation became unstoppable, and then wrote short stories such as *The Shattered Visage*, *Why Grandpa Won't Eat Sorghum Porridge*, *The Distant Wind and Sand*, and *Hatred*, all of which were included in the collection of short stories *Hatred* in 1937. The long novel *The Ocean of the Land* was also published at this time. Since then his talent began to be noticed.

After the August 13th Incident in 1937, Duanmu Hongliang went into exile from Shanghai to Wuhan, and then went to teach at Shanxi Linfen National Revolutionary University. After the fall of Linfen, he returned to Wuhan and married Xiao Hong in April 1938 in Wuhan. In August, he went to Chongqing, edited the *Digest Supplement*, and taught at Fudan University in

Chongqing. During his stay in Chongqing, he wrote a long story *Xindu Sidelights* and *The Great River*, a medium-length novel *Jiangnan Scenery* and some short stories. In early 1940, he and Xiao Hong were invited to Hong Kong. Duanmu Hongliang edited *the Great Era Literary Collection* for the Times Bookstore and edited the magazine *Times Literature*. During this period, he wrote *The Prehistory of Horqin* and a long novel *The Great Era* (unfinished), etc.

After the death of Xiao Hong in 1942, Duanmu Hongliang left Hong Kong and returned to Guilin, edited *Literature and Art Magazine*, wrote the second part of *Horqin Banner Grassland*, and composed the Peking Opera *The Tale of Hong Fu* and the dramas *Lin Daiyu*, *Qingwen*, and *Anna Karenina*, and so on. At the end of 1944, he became the director of the Li Newspaper Office in Zunyi and wrote *The Most Ancient Treasures*. In the winter of 1945, he traveled from Chongqing to Wuhan to edit a supplement of *Dagangbao* titled *Dajiang*. In the fall of 1947, he went to Changsha to become the head of the academic department of Shuiluzhou Music School. In 1948, he went to Shanghai to edit the magazines *Qiushi* and *Silver Critique*. In the fall, he went to Hong Kong. In August 1949, he returned to Beijing. He first participated in the land reform in the suburbs of Beijing, then prepared the Beijing Federation of Literary and Art Circles, and served as Deputy Director of the Creative Department, Deputy Director of the Publication Department, and Deputy Secretary General of the Circle. Taking Shougang as his living base, he worked with the workers to complete the history of the factory *The Ode of Steel*. In September 1952, he joined the Communist Party of China. Then he specialized in literary creation and became vice-chairman of the Beijing Writer's Association.

After the downfall of the Gang of Four, he wrote a long historical figure novel, *Cao Xueqin*.

Introduction to Works

Among the "Northeastern Writers in Exile", Duanmu Hongliang is a very famous one. His unique style of creation attracted millions of admirers which makes him another outstanding writer who represents the artistic achievements of the "Northeastern Writers in Exile" after Xiao Hong and Xiao Jun.

At the age of twenty-one, he wrote his famous long novel Horqin Banner Grassland. With his outstanding talent, he made his way into the Shanghai literary circle with his chilling depictions of the stark reality of rural Northeast China. He has been a writer for half a century, creative and unrestrained in writing, leaving behind fruitful creations. Among the northeastern writers, amazingly, he not only has a larger number of works, but also made comprehensive artistic attainments. He has created a total of five long novels, two short story collections, a mid length collection, as well as over 100 short stories and essays that have not yet been included in the collections, and more than 30 poems. He wrote modern dramas, Peking Operas, Criticism Operas, and film scripts. In addition, he published lyrics, paintings, calligraphies, translation works, and more than forty political and artistic essays. Like Xiao Hong, Duanmu Hongliang was one of the "Northeastern Writers in Exile" who showed his talent and diligence in writing.

Duanmu Hongliang's whole life creation can be summarized into four main periods: from 1933 to 1937 in Beijing and Shanghai. His main works include the long novel *Horqin Banner Grassland*, *The Ocean of the Land*, short stories *The Raging Current of the Hunhe River*, *Melancholy of the Cilu Lake*, *Why Grandpa Won't Eat Sorghum Porridge*, *The Distant Wind and Sand* and other famous pieces. From 1938 to 1940 in Chongqing. His major works include the long novel *The Great River*, *Xindu Sidelights*, and short novels. From 1942 to 1944 in Guilin, his main works were dramas, short novels and commentaries. After 1949 in Beijing, his main works were dramas, essays, commentaries, long novel *Cao Xueqin*, and so on.

The earliest establishment of Duanmu Hongliang's position in the literary world was his influential long novel *Horqin Banner Grassland*. The importance of this novel to him is just like that of *The Field of Life and Death* to Xiao Hong.

Horqin Banner Grassland shows the historical life of the Northeast society on the eve of the Mukden Incident. The novel exposes the cruel exploitation of the farmers by the landlords and shows the awakening of the farmers' class consciousness and anti-Japanese consciousness through the dispute over the land between the Ding family, the first owner of the grassland, and the farmers and herdsmen in the grassland. The theme of the work is the decline of the landlord class and the rise of a new farmer force represented by Dashan, who represents the rebirth of the grassland.

Duanmu Hongliang had a strong sensitivity to the times. He grasped the lifeblood of the landlord class in Northeast China - the land, around which he depicted the characters and made the plot full of twists and turns. He said: "I try to view many people and things reflected on this grassland from the perspectives of production relations and the possession and distribution of materials." [1] Wang Yao commented in *The Manuscript of Chinese new Literature History*: "The noblest wealth here is the land. The land can dominate everything. ... ... Since land is the source of revenue, those who hold it become the center of the society. The landlords were the center, and many systems, crimes, and unwritten laws were made, invented, and enforced by them. ... The author explains the reasons for the collapse of the feudal landlords from the confrontation between the farmers and the landlords. " "The book uses the farmers' struggle over the land to write about the decline of the landlords and the grassland. "The moment of the decline of the old-fashioned landlords and the awakening of the young generation of farmers, on the eve of

1 Duanmu Hongliang: *Conversations at the Book Window, Literary Book Window*, Issue 5, May 15, 1981.

the Mukden Incident, is of unusual significance. Coming events cast their shadows before them, in the grassland, in the closely following the Mukden Incident, who can become the master of this grassland, and who can master the grassland's future, the implied answer in the book is obvious.

The novel shows a magnificent picture with its majestic grandeur. Over the vast grassland, various characters live here, and new ideas and old cultures had their up and downs. The miserable life of the farmers, the difficult manual works, the prying eyes of the Japanese invaders, the uncertainty of the national bourgeoisie, the coexistence of the rough and the delicate, the absurdity and the civilization, constitute the history and reality of the grassland. Under such a huge historical environment, all the people and the things are active. The grassland in the author's mind has a profound meaning, and the author's creative intention is expressed through the grassland's prosperity and decay. As Ba Ren commented, the author has made the grassland "upright". The grassland becomes the embodiment of the specific historical environment of Northeast China.

Another prominent aspect of the novel is the portrayal of the landlord class in Northeast China, especially the portrayal of the spiritual world of Ding Ning, a "newcomer" in the landlord class, pointing out the duality of Ding Ning's character and his inevitable end as a martyr of the declining class. This is a work of autobiography, and Ding's house is essentially Duanmu Hongliang's own Cao's house. His thorough understanding of the family life and the rural environment since his childhood made him skillful in such a field.

Horqin Banner Grassland is also clearly influenced by the Russian writer Lev Tolstoy's *Resurrection*. It was published in Shanghai in the 1930s, and was like a companion volume of Mao Dun's famous novel *Midnight*, which depicted the fate of China's national capitalist industry in the 1930s. Together they drew a microcosm of China's semi-colonial and semi-feudal society, which is another aspect of the novel's contemporary significance.

Other works of Duanmu Hongliang, such as *The Ocean of the Land*, are still centered on the theme of land in Northeast China, depicting how the farmers reclaimed their land from the Japanese invaders. Another long novel, *The Great River*, depicts the growth of two anti-Japanese fighters, Tieling and Li Sanmazi. The scene of a difficult march of an anti Japanese army illustrates the arduousness of the anti Japanese cause and the belief that victory is inevitable. His short stories focus on the suffering of the farmers in the Northeast and the portrayal of their characters. *The Raging Current of the Hunhe River*, *Melancholy of the Cilu Lake*, *Why Grandpa Won't Eat Sorghum Porridge*, etc., all of them make people feel the vigorous vitality of the northeastern farmers' hearts beating in their weakened bodies. Duanmu Hongliang is good at portraying women, especially the abused and oppressed women of the lower class. Xiangling, Brother Chun and Shuisui in *Horqin Banner Grassland*, Xingzi in *The Ocean of the Land*, and Shuiqinzi in *The Raging Current of the Hunhe River* are all very touching.

Among the "Northeastern Writers in Exile", Duanmu Hongliang's artistic temperament is closer to that of Xiao Hong. His works are more delicate than vigorous, more subtle than majestic, and although there is no lack of forceful beauty, they are more melodious and euphonious, shaping a heavenly mood. If Xiao Jun is overwhelming, then Duanmu Hongliang and Xiao Hong are more elegant and free-spirited. The graceful demeanor, refined and fluent writing style, warm yet bold personality, and extensive knowledge structure constitute his unique creative style.

Duanmu Hongliang's creative style is complex, with radical aesthetic ideals often accompanied by a melancholic atmosphere. The powerful force always gives people a delicate and tender feeling. Like the white poplar in the north is accompanied by the soft willow in the south, which has both a carefree and soft jade fragrance. They correspond to each other in a contradictory way, forming a distinct, rich, and colorful style. His artistic state of mind seems to be a mixture of roughness and delicacy. Sima Changfeng commented on *Horqin Banner Grassland* in *The History of Chinese New Literature* that it was "a novel that is not easy to read. There are many serious shortcomings, but in some aspects, the achievements are remarkable and unparalleled in the world". And he talked about the language he used to write has two features, one was the natural and fluent Northeastern dialect, and the other was the convoluted European accent. "Suddenly flowing like water, but suddenly sinking into mud." This means that Sima noticed the contradictions and complexity of Duanmu Hongliang's creation.

Duanmu Hongliang is very good at environmental description, by which he can set the atmosphere of the whole story, which is prominent in his short stories. He also often uses certain techniques of film art to unfold the plot, such as the use of montage shots, tracking, temporal and spatial transformations, gradual and fading of characters, etc., fully mobilizing readers' vision and expanding a richer artistic space. His early works were thick and majestic, with a strong sense of the times. Later, when he was stranded in Hong Kong and the Mainland, the contemporary notes of his works were weakened for a while, and his ideological content tended to be "soft". However, it should be noted that even these works, which are considered to be weakened in ideology, are outstanding in their artistic value. Whether it is the knowledge and skills, or the delicate feelings, all of them are fascinating. This is the unique charm of Duanmu Hongliang.

Chapter 8 Shu Qun: The Hearts of People Who Lost Their Homeland

Biography

Shu Qun (1913-1989), Manchu, originally named Li Shutang, formerly known as Li Xudong, pen name Hei Ren. Born on September 20, 1913, in a working-class family in Harbin, Heilongjiang Province.

At the age of seven, he was enrolled in the Xiying Elementary School in Acheng County (now Acheng District, Harbin). Later, he moved with his family to Yimianpo and enrolled in the Second Elementary School in Zhuhe County (now Shangzhi City). At the age of fifteen, he was admitted to Harbin NO.1 Senior High School, where he became acquainted with a North Korean child, and his homeroom teacher was a Soviet girl, who later became the prototype of the characters in Shu Qun's novel *Children Without a Homeland*.

After graduating from junior high school in 1930, he was admitted to a free mercantile marine school in Harbin, but after only half a year of study, he dropped out due to financial difficulties and went to work as a Russian interpreter for the navigation Bureau.

In 1932, he joined the Third International, joined the Communist Party of China in September, and began to publish poetry and essays. He engaged in literary activities with Sai Ke, Luo Feng, Jin Jianxiao, Xiao Jun, Xiao Hong and others in Harbin, and was also an actor in the "Star Theater Troupe".

At the end of 1932, Shu Qun was sent to Taonan by the Party to serve as the head of the transportation station set up by the Third International. At the end of 1933, due to the hard struggle, he lost contact with the Party. At this time, the White Terror in Harbin intensified. In order to find the Party and further carry out anti-Japanese activities, Shu Qun, with the assistance of friends, arrived in Qingdao in early 1934. After establishing ties with the Party in Qingdao and getting married, Shu Qun gained a stable foothold. He then wrote a letter to call Xiao Jun and Xiao Hong, who were already in trouble in

Harbin. After they arrived in Qingdao, he lived with them at "No.1 Guanxiang Road".

In the autumn of that year, the Qingdao Party Organization was destroyed and Shu Qun was arrested. Due to the enemy's lack of control over his activities, he was only imprisoned for a few months. In prison, he wrote the famous short story *Children Without a Homeland.*

After his release, he was displaced several times and came to Shanghai. In 1935, he joined the Association of Chinese Left-Wing Writers in Shanghai and engaged in literary creation. After evacuating from Shanghai in 1937, he moved to Nanjing and Xi'an, and was then sent by the Organization to the headquarters of the Eighth Route Army as a war correspondent, and worked as a temporary secretary for Commander-in-Chief Zhu De.

In 1938, he went to Wuhan and co edited the publication *Battlefield* with Ding Ling. In 1940, he came to Yan'an and served as a teacher and head of the literature department at the Yan'an Luxun Academy of Fine Arts, as well as the editor in chief of the Fourth Edition of the *Jiefang Daily*. After the Rectification Movement, he spent nearly a year cultivating land in the 359th Brigade. In 1945, in Yan'an as the head of Northeast Performing Troupe, which came to the northeast in November. Since then, he has served as deputy director of the Propaganda Department of the Northeast Bureau of the Communist Party of China, vice president of Northeastern University, director of the Northeast Film Studio, and vice chairman of the Northeast Federation of Literary and Art Circles. After the founding of the People's Republic of China, he participated in the War to Resist US Aggression and Aid Korea in 1950. In 1951, he returned to China due to illness and went to Anshan to experience life. He served as the deputy secretary of the Party Committee of the Anshan Steel Rolling Mill. In 1953, he was transferred to Shenyang to specialize in literature and art. Later transferred to Beijing, served as deputy secretary general of the National Federation of Literary and Art Circles, director and secretary general of the National Writers Association. From 1955 onwards, he was wrongly criticized, and in 1958, he was wrongly labeled as an anti-Party member and then punished again. Then he served as deputy secretary of the Party Committee of the Benxi Second Iron Factory and deputy director of the Benxi Alloy Factory. In 1962, he was rehabilitated and restored to his former entitlement. That same year, the novel *The Generation* was published. In the Literary and Artistic Rectification Movement in 1963, Shu Qun's "rehabilitation verdict" was overturned, and he faced renewed criticism. During the Cultural Revolution, he was once again influenced and was arranged to live in the countryside in Muyuzi Commune, Huanren County, Benxi City for five years. In 1975, he returned to Benxi Niuxintai Mine from the countryside, and in 1978, he was formally recalled to Benxi City, where he served as the vice chairman of the Benxi City Federation of Literary and Art Circles. At the end of the year, he was transferred to the Institute of Literature of the Chinese Academy of Social Sciences in Beijing, and was finally completely rehabilitated. After that, he lived in Beijing for a long time. From 1979 onwards, in spite of his old age and illness, he published a dozen of short stories and memoirs, and edited literary publications. Among them, *The Untitled Story*, *Memories*, *The Yong Girl Chen*, Farewell, *The Night in Zhongnanhai*, *A Summary of the Great Man*, *The Beauty's Plea*, *The Banquet in Zaoyuan* and other works were all widely acclaimed.

On August 2, 1989, Shu Qun passed away in Beijing at the age of 76.

Introduction to Works

The peak period of Shu Qun's creativity was from 1936 to 1940. At that time, he entered the Shanghai literary circle with the short story *Children Without a Homeland*. It is his debut work, as well as his famous and representative work, like a shooting star, attracting people's eyes. The publication of the novel made Shu Qun spring into fame, becoming one of the most prominent writers among the "Northeastern Writers in Exile". Shu Qun's literary talent was particularly evident in the realm of short stories, a genre in which he demonstrated remarkable mastery.

The short story *Children Without a Homeland* was first published in May 1936 in the Shanghai's *Literature*, Volume 6, Number 5. The novel is based on Shu Qun's personal experience in the Middle East Railway's Children's School when he was a teenager, and describes the relationship and life encounters of three teenagers of different nationalities: the North Korean child Guoli, the Chinese child Gorbachev, and the Soviet child Guolisha. When the Northeast was occupied by Japan, Guoli and Gorbachev, who had lost their homeland, embarked on a journey to seek their homeland. The central character of the novel is the North Korean child, Guoli. When he was 10 years old, he came to Northeast China with his brother due to the fall of North Korea into Japanese colony, and lived in what they thought was "a free place". But soon, Northeast China also fell to Japan, and Guoli could not escape from the miserable fate of a "conquered people", and was seized for forced labor, enduring horrible physical torture and mental abuse. With flame of vengeance in his heart, he saw an opportunity to plunge a steel knife into the chest of a "devil". This is the revolt of the abused people, the revolt of the slaves. What the novel commends is the spirit of resistance of the oppressed nation, and celebrates the historical law that the people are invincible. The patriotic spirit of resistance against Japan is inherent in the novel, which constitutes the clear characteristics of the times.

Patriotism and internationalism are harmoniously united in this novel, which is another aspect of its deep historical significance. The word "homeland" is so important in the minds of Chinese child Gorbachev and North Korean child Guoli. Gorbachev sympathizes with Guoli's situation, he saw today's Northeast China from yesterday's North Korea , and he deeply understands the meaning of a homeland. When he saw the flag of his homeland lowered from the roof of the school, and the flag of another country, which he had never seen before, was raised, he could not help but painfully " fling himself against the glass of the storeroom " to take another look at his homeland's flag which had been thrown "under the corner". From then on, his heart always hoped for the raise of the flag of his homeland which became a symbol of his country. In order to seek freedom, he and Guoli were determined to escape from the den and embrace their homeland. Returning to his homeland has become a spiritual and emotional support for him, a goal for all his actions, and a bridge for his spiritual communication with Guoli. The novel also profoundly portrays the image of Soviet female teacher Sudova, who had already begun building socialism. She comes from a fresh land, symbolizing a new calling and a new vision. She said to Guoli with deep meaning: "In the future, it will be the responsibility of Koryo (North Korea) people as well as you to raise the flag of your homeland on their land." The friendship between the people of China, North Korea and the Soviet Union, linked by the "flag of the homeland", integrated the spirit of patriotism and internationalism of different nations into one. The profound theme has opened up the height that the literature of the same period has not yet reached, and the ingenious conception is also refreshing.

The arrangement of the novel to depict the fate of the North Korean child Goli in the historical background of Northeast China has profound implication. The author's purpose is very clear, that is, to remind people: what fate will one have if they lose their homeland! Published on the eve of the National War of Resistance against Japanese Aggression, this novel, which reflects the spirit of patriotism and internationalism, has prominent significance. Just as Zhou Yang commented: "In a recent novel called *Children Without a Homeland*, we are touched by the young protagonist's passionate nostalgia for the homeland flag. However, this is not a narrow-minded patriotism, but a natural harmony of internationalist spirit. [1]Zhou Libo said that the reason why this novel was welcomed by a large number of readers when it was published was "because he described the driving force of the national liberation movement that is needed now"[2].

Children Without a Homeland captures a corner of social life in the Northeast China and extends a deep reflection on the historical destiny of the nation. There is an air of simplicity throughout the text, with sincere and natural sentiment. It is no wonder that Zhou Libo considered that it "surpasses the general level of our literature in both artistic achievements as well as the depth and breadth of reflection of the times"[3]. This novel is the crystallization of the writer's life and feelings, and the author's artistic skills are quite sophisticated, making people feel that even as a debut work, it is quite mature.

Shu Qun's early short story creations were characterized by a wide range of themes, deep exploration of themes, deep focus on reflecting real life, and its persistence of following a solid path of realism. Before 1940 , he had published three collections of short stories, *Children Without a Homeland (1936)*, *Battlefields (1937)*, and *Beyond the Sea (1940)*.

In *Battlefield*, he depicted more of the horror of the society after the fall of Northeast China, and the reality of people being captured and bullied by the Japanese invaders. *The Country Girl* describes a tragic scene in the countryside: there is no smoke from kitchen chimneys in the village, no sound of livestock, all the men have run away, only the disabled and the old woman remain, and the "young girls" have their faces smeared with wood ash... This has become a world of silence. The story of *Wedding Night* is about a rural girl who rushes to her in laws' house to get married in order to avoid the enemy's

---

[1] Zhou Yang : *Regarding National Defense Literature,* inaugural issue of *Literary World* in 1936

[2] Zhou Libo: *A Review of Fiction Creation in 1936- A Year of Abundance*, *Guangming Journal*, Volume 2, Issue 2, 1937.

[3] Zhou Yang : *Regarding National Defense Literature,* inaugural issue of *Literary World* in 1936.

brutality. However, on their wedding night, the enemy found her and captured her husband. This tragic fate was a true portrayal of the rural areas in Northeast China at that time. *The Painter* and *The First Project of an Engineer* show the tragic fate of intellectuals in exile. In addition, *Amidst Hardship*, *The Orphans*, *Slaves and Masters* all these novels expose the enemy's brutality and the nightmare reality of the people being ravaged and persecuted from different perspectives.

The novel *Life in the Water* exposes the new disasters caused by the Koumintang Government's non resistance policy from another angle. On one side is the crowd who are used to playing at dusk in July, living a life of intoxication and dreams and seeking pleasure there; On one side is a 15 year old girl who makes a living by selling flowers, struggling to pick flowers in the water. On one side is a "peach colored embroidered patterned" window cap "floating out gentle and fragrant air"; On one side were homeless children begging for food by the roadside under the oppressive and heavy atmosphere. The stark contrast, paired with each other, calls for people's conscience and contemplation on the fate of their homeland. In *Scars of the Homeland*, depicts a group of bored, numb, fun-seeking 'onlookers' teasing, ridiculing, and harming a wounded soldier. The novel tells people that the "scars" of the homeland lie more in the people's mind through the depiction of abnormal psychology and numb souls of "the onlookers". The novel tells people that to awaken and educate the public, they should never stop at empty slogans.

Shu Qun also wrote many works based on anti-Japanese soldiers, depicting the heroic fights of the people against the enemy. *Battlefield* depicts a small anti-Japanese squa's spirit of unity and mutual assistance as well as the determination to stick to the 'battlefield' to the end in an exceptionally difficult environment under a desolate and desolate atmosphere. *The Oath* depicts the growth and initial failure of the anti-Japanese forces, emphasizing the determination of the soldiers to fight to the death against Japan. *The Tribute of the Songhua River* depicts the heroic act of soldiers on a warship on the

Songhua River, who swore to die not to be slaves to the enemy and shared the fate with the ship, demonstrating the resolute resistance of patriotic officers and soldiers in the Kuomintang Army against the Japanese invasion. *A Part of Short Song of Blood* depicts a touching story of an anti-Japanese soldier who sacrificed his love for the interests of his country. The medium-length novel *The Old Solider* depicts the tumultuous experience of patriotic soldiers facing national disasters through the plight of the "old soldier" Zhang Hai, who began to awaken in the national disaster, praising the burning flames of resistance of the Chinese nation.

In addition, there are other better novels such as *Sparks in the Desert*, *Mongolian Night* and *Xiao Ling*. The first two novels depict the awakening of Mongolian brothers' anti-Japanese consciousness, filled with a unique grassland atmosphere. The latter portrays a young growing up patriotic student , with distinctive characters and a fresh, endearing tone. In addition, it is worth mentioning that the novels *The Oath*, *Being Human*, *Neighborhood*, *The Dead and the Undead*, *The Bachelor* and other novels have a strong sense of the times. Shu Qun's short story writing is extremely brilliant. First of all, he pays great attention to reflecting the real life and consciously follows the times. He never cobbled characters together or fabricated plots, but instead he depicted ordinary people and events around him in the context of the ongoing anti Japanese war, in the context of Chinese society and the reality of Northeast China, making them appear real and realistic. Secondly, he pays great attention to character development, especially the changes of actions and ideological of the characters, following a reasonable, convincing, and historically consistent trajectory of character development. He has successfully portrayed many characters with different identities and personalities, including workers, farmers, urban poor, poor students, patriotic merchants, fighters in the anti-Japanese army, young mothers, wandering teenagers, as well as the Han nationally, and ethnic minorities... They constitute a group of characters covering all social strata. The numerous figures in this historical stage have presented us with an active three-dimensional stage, which has the value of understanding society and history. In addition, Shu Qun's works often give people a spiritual impact and ideological education in their understated and plain narratives. When you first read his novels, you feel relaxed and comfortable, but as time goes on, your emotions become heavier and heavier. Your emotions will often resonate with his narration.

Among the "Northeastern Writers in Exile", Shu Qun is a master of short stories. His medium and long stories are less influential than his short stories. His writing style combines elegance and simplicity, with lightness and solemnity complementing each other, creating a delicate and colorful style. Unfortunately, it’s very regretful that, his creative time was affected and his talent was not fully exposed due to his difficult life and unfair encounters.

Chapter 9 Luo Feng and Bai Lang: A Couple Goes Through Thick and Thin Together

Biography

Luo Feng (1909-1991), originally named Fu Naiqi, used pen names Luo Hong, Ke Ning, Luo Xun, and Peng Bo, was born on December 13, 1909, in Sujiatun, Shenyang, Liaoning Province.

Luo Feng was originally from Penglai, Shandong Province. His Grandfather Fu Jinglin brought his family to Shenyang during the journey to the Northeast. His father worked as a letter carrier and clerk. Luo Feng started studying in a private school at the age of seven and entered Fengtian Xiaonanguan Provincial First Normal School Affiliated Mofan Primary School at the age of eight. Because of the family's poverty, he grew up fast and helped the family to do the work at a very young age. He was both diligent and gifted, maintaining outstanding academic performance throughout.

When Luo Feng was three years old, the Luo family moved to Daxiguan in Shenyang. From then on, he often went to his aunt's (Bai Lang's mother) house, and became childhood sweethearts with his cousin Bai Lang.

Bai Lang (1912-1990), originally named Liu Donglan, pen names Liu Li, Yi Bai, etc., was born on August 2, 1912, in Shenyang, Liaoning Province. She was gifted and had a strong desire to learn, and was enrolled in elementary school at the age of six. Bai Lang's grandfather's name was Liu Ziyang, a famous traditional Chinese medicine practitioner, so was his father. Later, Bai Lang's family and the Luo Feng's family moved to Qiqihar, Heilongjiang Province. Liu Ziyang made a living as a doctor and also served as a military doctor director in Wu Junsheng's army. Soon after, Bai Lang's father passed away, his grandfather lost his job, plunging the Liu family into dire straits.

In Qiqihar, Luo Feng's family and Bai Lang's family live in the same courtyard, so they have more opportunities to contact witch each other. From then on, their emotional bond grows deeper with each passing day. Bai Lang's mother also loved the smart and sensible Luo Feng, and betrothed her eldest daughter Liu Dongzhi to him. Unexpectedly, Dongzhi passed away at the age of 16, and Liu's mother then betrothed her youngest daughter Bai Lang to him. In the autumn of 1929, the two finally became husband and wife, and they fell in love with each other.

At the age of 14, Luo Feng was admitted to the First Middle School of Heilongjiang Province. At that time, Bai Lang was studying at the First Women's Normal School of Heilongjiang Province. After graduating from the middle school, Luo Feng was unable to continue his education due to his family's financial difficulties, so he stayed at home and immersed himself in reading, coming into contact with a large number of new literary works, which led to his increasingly progressive thinking. In 1928, he was admitted to the Training Institute of the Huhai Railway. During his studies, he secretly joined a reading group organized by Hu Rongqing, an underground member of the Communist Party of China, and began writing new poetry. In 1929, the first industrial branch of the CPC in North Manchuria—the Special Branch of the Huhai Railway of the CPC Central Committee—was established. Luo Feng joined the Party and served as the propaganda officer for the branch. From then on, he began to engage in the progressive literary and artistic work of the Party. In 1930, he launched the publication *Knowledge and Action Monthly* among the employees of the Huhai Railway. In 1932, Luo Feng became the secretary of the Special Branch and was later transferred to serve as the propaganda committee member of the Daowai District Committee in Harbin. Together with underground Party member Jin Jianxiao and others, he published newspapers and magazines. Under the direction of the Manchurian Provincial Committee, he carried out revolutionary literary and artistic activities in Harbin.

Influenced by Luo Feng, Bai Lang also found a meaningful path in life. After their marriage, she was drawn to the grand political ideals and gradually immersed herself in progressive activities. She joined the secret progressive organization "Anti-Japanese Alliance," becoming Luo Feng's like-minded revolutionary companion.

In April 1933, Bai Lang was admitted as a journalist for the *International Association Newspaper*. Not long after, he resigned from the position and took over as the Deputy Editor of the *International Association Newspaper* in October, embarking on her literary career. She and Xiao Hong entered the literary world of Harbin almost simultaneously and had close exchanges with each other. For a moment, a group of young Northeastern writers such as Xiao Jun, Xiao Hong, Shu Qun, Jin Jin, and Lin Jue gathered around Luo Feng and Bai Lang. They held secret gatherings and even organized the Star Theater Troupe to promote progressive literature and art in Harbin.

At this time, Bai Lang began to publish novels in the supplement of the *International Association Newspaper*, mainly including *The Rebel Son* and *The Terrifying Aperture*. Luo Feng has published the one-act drama *It's Late Now*, the medium-length novel *The Scattered Stars*, and the short stories *Testimony* and *Victory*. They are young, active, and full of vitality, and have gone through an unforgettable period.

In June 1934, Luo Feng was arrested in Harbin. He persisted in his struggle in prison and never exposed his identity. A year later, through the efforts of the Organization, they were were released from prison. Luo Feng and Bai Lang left Harbin and came to Shanghai at the end of 1935 where they started a new life of fighting.

In 1936, Luo Feng joined the Association of Chinese Left-Wing Writers in Shanghai and by the end of the year, he published a collection of short stories titled *By the Hulan River*. Then he went on to create more short stories such as *The Seventh Pit*, the medium-length novels including *The Return* and *Mo Yun and Lieutenant Hanermo*. Among these, *The Seventh Pit* received considerable acclaim and was translated into English for publication in *International Literature*. Meanwhile, Bai Lang wrote short stories like *By the Yiwalu River* and *A Strange Kiss*. From then on, the couple became prominent

Northeastern writers attracting much attention.

After the fall of Shanghai in 1937, Luo Feng and Bai Lang went to Wuhan. In the winter, Luo Feng traveled alone to Linfen in Shanxi to join the army, where he wrote the plays *Prisoners from Manchuria* and *The National Flag Flutters*, and collaborated on dramas such as *Taierzhuang* and *General Mobilization*. In 1938, Luo Feng and Bai Lang arrived in Chongqing. There, cultural figures established the Chinese Association of Literary and Art Circles for Resisting Enemy, with Luo Feng serving as secretary. In June 1939, Luo Feng and Bai Lang joined the Writer's Battlefield Visiting Group delving into the frontlines to experience and observe wartime life. In August, Bai Lang returned due to illness, while Luo Feng persisted for over a month, reaching as far as the Taihang Mountains. During this period, Luo Feng wrote the novella *Grain*, and Bai Lang wrote the medium-length novel *The Old Couple* and the diary-style reportage *Fourteen of Us*. At the beginning of 1941, Bai Lang and Luo Feng were arranged by the organization to leave Chongqing for Yan'an.

In Yan'an, Luo Feng was elected as the first Chairman of the Yan'an branch of the the Chinese Association of Literary and Art Circles for Resisting Enemy. In 1942, he served as a Standing Committee member and Secretary-General of the Shaanxi Gansu Ningxia Cultural Committee. Comrade Mao Zedong wrote several letters to Luo Feng, entrusting him to collect materials from the Yan'an literary and artistic circles for symposiums. In May 1942, Luo Feng and Bai Lang participated in the Yan'an Forum on Literature and Art.

In October 1941, Bai Lang served as the editor of the supplement of the *Jiefang Daily*, writing the novel *Record Outside the Prison* and the essay *Notes on Journey to the West* that depict his staying in Harbin . In 1942 and 1943, Luo Feng and Bai Lang went to study at the Third Department of the Central Party School. In the later stages of the Rectification Movement, they were both wrongly attacked by the "rescue movement" and were unjustly accused, resulting in Bai Lang's mental disorder for a period of time.

In the autumn of 1945, Luo Feng and Bai Lang, having recovered from illness, left Yan'an for Northeast China. By the end of the year, they were working in the Jijiang Military District. In 1946, Luo Feng served as a standing committee member of the Propaganda and Culture Committee of the Northeast Bureau of the Central Committee of the Communist Party of China, acting chairman of the Northeast Culture Association, and vice president of the Harbin Sino-Soviet Friendship Association, among other positions. After the founding of the People's Republic of China, he held various leadership roles in the cultural sector, including deputy minister and secretary-general of the Northeast People's Government's Ministry of Culture, member of the Northeast People's Government's Culture and Education Committee, vice chairman of the Northeast Federation of Literary and Art Circles, and first vice chairman of the Northeast Writers Association. In 1953, he led the "Repatriated Prisoners Interview Group," organized by the General Political Department and the Central Propaganda Department, to Kaesong and Panmunjom in Korea, where he attended the signing ceremony of the Korean Armistice Agreement.

After arriving in Northeast China, Bai Lang successively served as head of the supplements department of *Northeast Daily* and deputy editor-in-chief of *Northeast Literature and Art*. In 1950, she moved to Shenyang to focus on professional writing and participated in the War to Resist US Aggression and Aid Korea, visiting the front lines to gather material for her novel *Advancing on the Track*. In 1952, she joined a Chinese writers' delegation to visit Korea and attended the World Peace Congress in Vienna in December. In 1953, she participated in the World Women's Congress in Copenhagen, and in 1954, she attended the Asian Writers' Conference in India, engaging in a series of international cultural exchange activities. During this period, she also wrote the acclaimed medium length novel *For a Better Tomorrow*.

In 1955, Luo Feng and Bai Lang were wrongly identified as members of the anti Party group, and later labeled as " the rightists", repeatedly criticized.

In 1958, he went to Fuxin Coal Mine in Liaoning Province to participate in labor. In 1963, he moved to Jinxian County, Liaoning Province (now merged into Jinpu New District, Dalian City). During this period, Luo Feng wrote a reportage titled *The Train is Moving* reflecting the industrial front. During the Cultural Revolution, they were criticized and physically and mentally devastated, and Bai Lang's body gradually deteriorated. This couple has been struggling together, going through the most difficult years, and Luo Feng has never admitted to the "charges" imposed on him. After crushing the Gang of Four, they were thoroughly exonerated and cleared of years of injustice. Later, he moved to Beijing and picked up the pen that had been delayed for many years in his twilight years.

Introduction to Works

Luo Feng and Shu Qun are similar in that most of their works were created in the early stages of the War of Resistance Against Japanese Aggression and are predominantly short stories. However, their temperaments and styles are quite different. It can be said that Luo Feng appears more robust. This may be determined by his personal temperament, as well as the fact that he joined the Party earlier and was more politically mature. Luo Feng's unyielding character was once celebrated among Northeastern writers as the famous "tough guy."

Luo Feng's influential representative work from the 1930s is the short story *The Seventh Pit*.

The Seventh Pit depicts the city of Shenyang just after the September 18 Incident, where a shoemaker named Geng Da is forced by Japanese soldiers to dig pits to bury his own compatriots alive (among them even his uncle). When he realizes that the seventh pit he is digging is intended for himself, he can no longer suppress the fury of resistance in his heart and swings his shovel at a

Japanese soldier beside him. The story is like a , vivid and realistic witness record, with the bloody reality conveying the profound disaster that the Mukden Incident brought to the people of the Northeast China. After its publication, the work shocked its readers. Another short story, *By the Hulan River*, tells of a Japanese garrison stationed at the Hulan River bridge, which, to guard against the Volunteer Army, captured a young cowherd and brutally kills him two days later. Villagers only find the bones of the cow and the child's body in the grass. Through these common occurrences in the Northeast China at the time, the author exposes the enemy's cruelty and portrays the destruction of ordinary people in Northeast China. Luo Feng often skillfully processed what he witnessed in life, and his narrative style is simple and natural. The author's subjective emotions are hidden and not overtly expressed; everything is revealed through the work, through the actions and fates of the characters.

Luo Feng's short story collection *Crossing* was published in 1940, including 15 of the author's stories, which represents the culmination of his creative work during this period. *Repeat Offender* portrays a normal citizen named Xie Yuan who, in the occupied Northeast China society, is unable to find a job and faces obstacles everywhere. Despite harboring naive fantasies, he finds himself at a dead end. The story moves from class conflict to national conflict, subtly critiquing and suggesting a path of resistance, prompting deep reflection. *Three Hundred and Seven and One* tells of an old man who found his lost grandson, only to discover that he is about to be transported to Japan to be trained as a tool of the enemy. The old man resolutely hides poison in a cake for his grandson and tragically consumes the other half himself, fully demonstrating the integrity of the Chinese nation. Other stories like *Wan Dahua*, *Deserted Village*, and *The Death of Dr. Zuo* are all sobering and possess profound ideological depth.

Luo Feng has a considerable number of short stories, such as *In Prison*, *Wreath*, *Kosov's Hair*, *and Five Minutes*, as well as medium-length novels like

The Return and *Mo Yun and Lieutenant Hanermo*, all of which are quite commendable. His works possess a peculiar and robust beauty, tragic yet not wounding, sorrowful yet stirring, with an inner radiance of masculine vigor and the unyielding spirit of the nation, carrying a weight of immense significance. In addition, Luo Feng also wrote the long poem The *Monument*, dramas like *The Confrontation of Two Camps*, *It's Late Now* and *Passing the Shanhai Pass*, the reportage *The Train is Moving*, and numerous poems, essays, and critiques, demonstrating his diligence and prolific output. However, what leaves the deepest impression are his short stories.

Bai Lang was a diligent writer, and the quantity of her works is no less than that of Luo Feng. Her writings often express her personal experiences and feelings from her revolutionary activities, documenting the real struggles of the various periods she lived through. She paid special attention to and was sensitive to women's issues. In *Four Years*, there is the distressed and wavering young woman Dai Jia; in *Precious Memories*, there is the revolutionary mother; in *The Rebellious Son*, there is the tragic poor man's daughter Yin Na; in *Life and Death*, there is the elderly aunt; in *A Strange Kiss*, there is the strong and loving female soldier Li Hua; and especially in *For a Happy Tomorrow*, there is Shao Yumei, who grows from a beggar child to a model CPC member. These characters are all vividly portrayed and full of life, forming a gallery of female images under the theme of Northeastern literature. Bai Lang's most outstanding early work is the short story *Life and Death*. It depicts the process of spiritual awakening of a female prison guard "old aunt" under the influence of revolutionaries. In the end, the old aunt chooses to sacrifice herself gloriously for the patriots, showing the awakening of the Northeast people's resistance against Japan and the righteous spirit of the revolutionaries. The story is tightly structured, with simple language and a bright tone. The character of the old aunt has the image of the mother in Gorky's work *Mother*. Other notable works include the short stories *By the Yiwalu River*, *The Visit*, *Precious Memories*, *Punishment on Women*, *Under the*

Wheels, medium-length novel *The Old Couple*, and the essay collection *Notes on Journey to the West*, all of which have distinctive features.

After the founding of the People's Republic of China, Bai Lang's most famous work is the medium-length novel *For a Happy Tomorrow*. The novel showcases the enthusiasm and spiritual outlook of the people in the early days of the People's Republic of China as they built socialism, celebrating the model figures who grew from workers. Bai Lang also wrote some travel essays that are smooth, passionate, and brimming with the spirit of the times. Speaking of her own works, Bai Lang said, "I've been writing for half a lifetime, and it's all been 'potboilers.'" (Bai Ying *Biography of Bai Lang*) This is certainly humble, but it also reflects the lack of refinement in the works.

Chapter 10 Luo Binji: The Unrestricted Spring in Beiwang Garden

Biography

Luo Binji (1917–1994), originally named Zhang Pujun, was born on February 12, 1917, in Hunchun County, Jilin Province, into a family of small business owners with ancestral roots in Pingdu, Shandong Province. His childhood was marked by poverty, and he was repeatedly forced to drop out of elementary school to help with farm work at home. In 1933, he went to Jinan to attend middle school and also audited classes at Peking University. However, due to financial difficulties, he had to take break from studies and returned to Hunchun in the summer of 1935. During this period, Luo Binji was exposed to many new literary works and developed a thirst for knowledge. He once considered studying in the Soviet Union, but this plan did not materialize. Subsequently, he went to Harbin and enrolled in Jinghua College to study Russian where he met Jin Jianxiao. Through Jin Jianxiao, Luo learned that Xiao Jun and Xiao Hong, who had left Harbin and become famous left-wing writers in Shanghai. Inspired by their success, Luo Binji resolved to dedicate himself to pursing new literature.

In May 1936, Luo Binji fled from Harbin to Shanghai, where he began immersing himself in writing his first novel, *On the Borderline*, marking the beginning of his literary career. In June 1937, he published his debut work, *Gorky Lives Forever in Our Hearts*, in Shanghai *Oriental Express*. In October 1937, his work *A Day in Great Shanghai* was published in *Call to Arms*, earning acclaim for its delicate portrayal of the lives of Shanghai citizens as the War of Resistance Against Japanese Aggression approached. After the fall of Shanghai, Luo went to eastern Zhejiang to engage in anti-Japanese propaganda and joined the Communist Party of China.

In 1939, Luo Binji served as the editor of the publication *War Flag* in Shaoxing. In 1940, he went to the headquarters of the New Fourth Army in southern Anhui. By October, he returned to Zhejiang but lost contact with the Organization, forcing him to drift alone to Guilin, where he devoted himself to writing. During this period, he was highly prolific, writing the medium-length novel *The East Battlefield Special Forces* and *Wu Feiyou*, the reportage *A Busy Summer*, and the short story *Loneliness* and other works. He also published his novel *On the Borderline*. Soon after, he went to Hong Kong, where he published the short story *A Stubborn Man* in *Bitan*, a magazine edited by Mao Dun. During this time, he also cared for the ailing Xiao Hong until her death on January 22, 1942. Afterward, he left Hong Kong and returned to Guilin. Later, he wrote *A Biography of Xiao Hong*.

From 1942 to 1944, he published the novel *Childhood* and the famous short story collection *Spring in Beiwangyuan* in Guilin.

In May 1944, Luo Binji arrived in Chongqing. Shortly thereafter, he was arrested by the local Bureau of Investigation and Statistics of the Military Council and was only released after the intervention of the Chinese Association of Literary and Art Circles for Resisting Enemy. Following his release, he continued his literary work in the rural areas of Chongqing and published works in *Xinhua Daily*, a prominent newspaper in the city.

In 1946, Luo Binji moved to Shanghai, where he published the novel *Youth*, the script *May Lilac*, medium-length novel *The Evidence*, and the first two parts of his novel *The Family History of Jiang Buwei*—*Chaos* and *Haze* and other works.

In 1947, Luo Binji was entrusted by the Party to investigate matters related to the Northeast Youth Association in Northeast China. However, he was unexpectedly arrested in Changchun and taken to Shenyang, where he remained imprisoned until the liberation of Shenyang in the spring of 1949. After his release, he temporarily sought refuge in Hong Kong. In June of that year, he returned to Beijing from Hong Kong to attend the First National Literature and Arts Congress, where he was elected as an alternate member of the National Literary Association. Following this, he immersed himself in the lives of workers and farmers in Shandong Province. In 1950, he published *Zhang Baoluo's Memoirs* and was appointed vice chairman of the Shandong Provincial Federation of Literary and Art Circles. Later, he wrote the pingju *The Reconciliation of Sisters-in-Law* as well as short story collections such as *Old Wei Jun and Fangfang* and *Purchasing Station in Mountain*.

In 1953, he was transferred to Beijing to engage in film script creation. In 1958, he immersed himself in the lives in Mudanjiang area, Heilongjiang Province, and in 1962, he was transferred to the Beijing Federation of Literary and Art Circles to continue his professional creation. Affected by the Cultural Revolution, he was sent to a vocational school and transferred to the Beijing Museum of Culture and History in 1974.

After the Cultural Revolution, he persisted in creating and shifted his main focus to the research and verification of inscriptions on bronze. His *New Examination of Inscriptions on Bronze* is a work of great academic value after the founding of the People's Republic of China.

Introduction to Works

Luo Binji was one of the younger members of the "Northeastern Writers in Exile" and entered the literary circle slightly later than others. Most of his major works were written during the later period of the War of Resistance Against Japanese Aggression while he was in the southwestern hinterland. Nie Gannu described him as "an outstanding novelist of contemporary China" (Nie Gannu, *Gannu's Prose: Welcoming Luo Binji*). His works not only depict the anti-Japanese struggles of the people in Northeast China but also reflect life in the Kuomintang-controlled areas during the war. With vivid character portrayals, delicate and lively style, his writings possess a high degree of artistic quality.

On the Borderline is Luo Binji's first novel and one of the earliest works to depict the life of the anti-Japanese armed forces in Northeast China. The novel portrays people from various social stratum in H City, located on the border of Jilin Province, who join the Volunteer Army under the oppression of the Japanese Puppet Army. It also tells the story of how this anti-Japanese Volunteer Army overcomes internal conflicts and moves toward renewal. The novel sharply raises the issue of consolidating leadership within the anti-Japanese forces by relying on genuine anti-Japanese elements, making its ideological significance quite positive. However, the character portrayals are relatively weak, and the writing appears somewhat rushed. Mao Dun praised Luo for his skill in creating atmosphere but noted that the work still had moments of "immaturity."

The short story collection *Spring in Beiwang Garden* is Luo Binji's signature work, fully showcasing his unique talent as a writer. The collection includes a group of concise yet profound short stories, such as *An Incident in 1944*, *The Old Maid*, *Due to Love*, and *Ma Xiaogui and Captain Niu*, among which the most outstanding work is *Spring in Beiwang Garden*.

Spring in Beiwang Garden depicts the daily lives of a group of intellectuals living in Beiwang Garden in Guilin during the War of Resistance Against Japanese Aggression. The story vividly portrays their shabby, kind-hearted, pedantic, and lonely yet self strengthening personalities, addressing the realistic themes of intellectuals facing choices about their future during the war. The characters include a village head, Yang, a well-known politician who lives in a muddled and vulgar manner, indulging in remarking women after satiated with food and drink. Lin Meina, a painter's wife, is busy with trivial household chores and has long lost her desire to resist the Japanese. They are content with their mediocre lives, detached from the fiery struggles of the reality, and their so-called "happiness" is ethereal and meaningless. Zhao Renjie, an art teacher, is dissatisfied with the reality and unwilling to sink into despair, yet he is powerless to escape the pressures of life and his environment, thus spending his days "lost in thought in his gloomy room." He Dajie, a soldier, also struggles to break free from his life in a humble abode as his anti-Japanese passion gradually fades. However, the story is not entirely bleak; there are also pursuits of the soul, sparks of passion, and an unextinguished patriotic sentiment in some people’s heart. Many of these characters are from Northeast China, and they often call out for the North in their hearts and miss their homeland. They live in Beiwang Garden", and even name their child "Huai Bei". With a tone of compassion and sigh, the author analyses the complex souls of these wartime intellectuals, illustrating how their detachment from the fiery struggles of life has led to their sorrow. The warmth of the narrative carries reproach, and the forgiveness is tinged with satire, reflecting a profound contemplation of the social life in the Kuomintang-controlled areas. The story calls on those who have become depressed under the pressures of life to rise again. The strong critical spirit of reality and the a faint homesickness intertwine like an ink wash painting with balanced shades, leaving readers to ponder its profound theme.

In the short story *Fellow Villager—Kang Tiangang*, Kang Tiangang represents a different kind of progressive characters. He relentlessly pursues happiness and light, embodying an indomitable faith. He spends 20 years traversing mountains and valleys in search of ginseng, even sacrificing his life for this quest. The work celebrates this positive spirit of life and affirms this idealistic pursuit, which held significant realistic significance at the time. Similarly, in the drama *May Lilac*, the heroine Qu Xiufang also pursues the true meaning of life with unwavering commitment despite numerous setbacks. Like Kang Tiangang, she serves as a symbol of the author's hopes, standing in contrast to the fragile personalities depicted in Spring in Beiwang Garden. By giving these characters resolute and strong personalities, Luo Binji makes a deliberate choice against the backdrop of the anti-Japanese theme, highlighting their unwavering spirit in the face of adversity.

Luo Binji also wrote the autobiographical novel *Chaos*. The novel depicts the history and social customs of the Hunchun area in Jilin Province from the

Republic of China era to the May Fourth Movement, imbued with a strong local flavor. The writing is delicate, bright and gentle and gentle, with exquisite psychological portrayals of characters to showcase distinct artistic features. However, the work falls short in comprehensively capturing the life in that period, giving a sense of detachment from realistic struggle. The author's purist also appears somewhat indistinct, overly confined to the human’s life circle with limited vision.

Among the "Northeastern Writers in Exile," Luo Binji's style tends to be soft and gentle. His writing is delicate in texture, with a light and whimsical tone, and his characterizations are highly expressive. But the character's thoughts and personalities are slightly weak, appearing to be heavy and insufficient. This may be related to his extended stay in the southwestern hinterland during the War of Resistance Against Japanese Aggression. Duanmu Hongliang and Li Huiying also possess varying degrees of this' Southern style 'temperament. Even within the same group of "Northeastern Writers in Exile," there can be significant differences in their literary style and presentation.

Chapter 11 Ma Jia: The Crops in Liaohe Bay Have Risen up

Biography

Ma Jia (1910–2004), Manchu, was originally named Bai Yongfeng and also used the pen name Bai Xiaoguang. He was born on February 27, 1910, in Gongjiangpuzi Village, Xinmin, Liaoning Province. His grandfather, Bai Mingru, worked as a teacher in the countryside and he had a passion for literature, and held progressive ideas, which greatly influenced Ma Jia during his childhood. His father, Bai Qingxian, was a rural traditional Chinese medicine practitioner. From a young age, Ma Jia helped with farm work at home, which gives him a deep understanding of rural life in Northeast China.

At the age of seven, Ma Jia went to elementary school at local village. By the time he was 15, he enrolled at Wenhui Middle School in Xinmin County which was a missionary school established by British missionaries. Although Ma Jia disliked studying English and attending religious services, he developed a passion for literature and began to explore new literary works.

In the autumn of 1928, Ma Jia was admitted to the preparatory course of the Northeast University in Shenyang, where he studied in the Department of Education at the College of Education. That same year, he began his literary career, publishing his debut poem, *Song of Autumn*, in *Pingshi Daily* in Shenyang. During his time at the Northeast University, Ma Jia, along with some classmates, founded progressive literary journals such as *Northern Land* and *Tide of Fury*. He published works in newspapers and magazines, and his thought was more and more progressive. He admired left-wing writers like Lu Xun and Jiang Guangci.

On the eve of the Mukden Incident, Ma Jia moved to Peking and began a life of exile. Without any source of income, he faced extreme hardship, being both out of school and unemployed. Immersed in writing, he relied on meager earnings from his literary works to sustain himself. He published works in

Literary Monthly in Peking and *Guangming Journal* in Shanghai, and collaborated with friends to edit progressive publications such as *Literature Guide*, *Literary Style*, and *Dawn*. During this period, his major works included the medium-length novel *Before and After the Coronation* (also known as *Sparks in the Cold Night*), the long poems *Fire Sacrifice* and *March of the Old Capital*, and short stories like *Our Ancestors*, *Family Letters*, and *The Path of Revenge*. In 1935, he joined the Association of Chinese Left-Wing Writers in Peking and formally engaged in anti-Japanese and national salvation movement.

After the July 7th Incident in 1937, Peking fell, and Ma Jia was forced into exile once again. He traveled through Jinan, Nanjing, Kaifeng, and Xi'an, engaging in anti-Japanese propaganda. Later, through an introduction by Yu Yifu, he briefly worked in propaganda for the 181st Division. Soon after, he went to the Northwest Shanxi to join the work of the Mobilization Committee for War Efforts and served as the head of the work team in Guojia Village, Lan County. He also participated in the guerrilla forces led by Xu Fanting outside Yanmen Pass. In May 1938, he arrived in Yan'an.

After arriving in Yan'an, Ma Jia enrolled at the Northern Shaanxi Public School for studies. Upon graduation, he joined the Chinese Association of Literary and Art Circles for Resisting Enemy of the Border Region to focus on writing. From 1939 to 1941, he participated in the Cultural Troupe of the Eighth Route Army, traveling extensively through anti-Japanese base areas in central and southern Hebei, Shanxi-Chahar-Hebei, western Hebei, and western Shanxi. He moved with the troops and immersed himself in the life of the frontlines. In May 1941, he returned to Yan'an and engaged in professional writing at the Chinese Association of Literary and Art Circles for Resisting Enemy. Drawing from his experiences at the front, he wrote short stories and essays such as *General Xiao Ke at Malan*, *Courier Sun Lin*, *The Recipient of the Honor Flower*, and *Encampment*, which were published in Yan'an's *Guyu Journal* and *Jiefang Daily*. In 1945, his novel *The Hutuo River Basin*, which depicted life in the Shanxi-Chahar-Hebei anti-Japanese base area, was serialized in *Jiefang Daily*. While in Yan'an, Ma Jia joined the Communist Party of China, attended the Yan'an Forum on Literature and Art, and remained a diligent writer. In the later stages of the Rectification Movement, he studied at the Third Division of the Central Party School and was unjustly implicated during the "Rescue Campaign."

After the victory of the War of Resistance Against Japanese Aggression, Ma Jia traveled from Yan'an to Northeast China. He first worked briefly at the *Jin-Cha-Ji Daily* in Zhangjiakou, where he served as the editor of the supplement. In May 1946, he journeyed through the Horqin Grassland of Inner Mongolia to reach the liberated area of Qiqihar in North Manchuria. An encounter with enemy forces during his march across the grassland later inspired him to write the acclaimed medium-length novel *Unfading Flowers*, which vividly reflects this combat experience. The novel was translated into multiple foreign languages and received widespread acclaim, becoming Ma Jia's most celebrated work and establishing his reputation as a writer.

In June 1946, Ma Jia arrived in Jiamusi and was assigned to participate in the land reform in Huachuan County, where he served as deputy head of the work team and secretary of the district committee. His two-year experience in land reform inspired him to write the renowned medium-length novel *Ten Days in Jiangshan Village*, which vividly depicted the land reform movement in North Manchuria and received widespread acclaim. Afterward, Ma Jia returned to the Chinese Association of Literary and Art Circles for Resisting Enemy in Northeast China to continue his professional writing and participated in the First National Literature and Art Congress. In 1949, he was elected as a council member of the National Writers Association, and the following year, he became vice chairman of the Northeast Writers Association.

In 1950, Ma Jia participated in the War to Resist U.S. Aggression and Aid Korea, during which he wrote the novel *In the East of the Motherland*, reflecting the lives of Chinese People's Volunteers and civilian laborers. In

1951, he visited the Soviet Union. After the founding of the People's Republic of China, Ma Jia spent extended periods immersing himself in the lives of people in Xinmin County (now Xinmin City) and Gai County (now Gaizhou City) in Liaoning Province. In 1958, he moved with his family to Xinglong Commune in Xinmin County to deeply engage with rural life, and in 1963, he lived alone in Changshanzi Village in Xinmin County. In 1960, he published the novel *Red Fruits*, which depicted life during the agricultural collectivization movement.

Ma Jia served for a long time as the chairman of the Liaoning Provincial Writers Association and the chairman of the Liaoning Provincial Federation of Literary and Art Circles. His other works include the short stories *Shuanglong River*, *Crossing Dianzi Ridge*, and *The Radiance of New Life*, as well as essay collections such as *The Era of Happiness*, *The Rivers and Land of the Motherland*, and *Selected Essays of Ma Jia*.

Ma Jia was wrongly criticized during the Cultural Revolution. In 1969, he moved to the mountainous area of Ningcheng County, Inner Mongolia to settle down. Returned to Shenyang in 1973. After the Cultural Revolution, he regained his creative enthusiasm and wrote the poem *Yan'an Melody*, the short story *The Evergreen Mountains*, and numerous commentaries. In 1983, he wrote a historical masterpiece that reflected the struggles and lives of the people in the North. His autobiographical novel *The Record of the Northern Country* received widespread acclaim and won the first prize for literary creation from the Liaoning Provincial Government. In 1988, Ma Jia wrote a companion piece to the book, another novel titled *Blood Stains the Mountains and Rivers*. The success of these two works brought a brilliant flourish to his literary career in his later years.

Introduction to Works

Ma Jia holds a unique position among the Northeastern Writers in Exile. His literary career began early, and his body of work is extensive. With an exceptionally solid foundation in rural life in Northeast China, his writings consistently reflect the struggles and lives of the people there, making him a quintessential writer of the Northeast. His works matured over time, particularly in developing a distinctive artistic style imbued with the regional flavor of the Northeast, growing even more remarkable in his later years. He produced many notable works, the most famous being the medium length novel *Unfading Flowers*. Other renowned works include the medium length novel *Ten Days in Jiangshan Village* and the full-length novels *The Record of the Northern Country*, *Blood Stains the Mountains and Rivers*, and *Red Fruits*.

While his works are primarily novels, particularly excelling in medium-length and full-length novels, upon closer reading, one will see that the novels bear more traces of essay. He places great emphasis on characters' consciousness and psychology, as well as the language of his works, and excels at creating atmosphere. Rather than focusing on intricate plots, his writing embodies a natural simplicity, and heartfelt poetic quality, striving to achieve a simple artistic beauty that blends novel and essay into one.

Ma Jia was a diligent writer. During the War of Resistance Against Japanese Aggression, his works primarily depicted two major themes: rural life in Northeast China and the lives of soldiers and civilians in the anti-Japanese base areas in North China. His main works include the medium length novel *Sparks in the Cold Night*, the novel *The Hutuo River Basin*, the long poems *Fire Sacrifice* and *March of the Old Capital*, as well as numerous short stories.

Sparks in the Cold Night, originally titled *Before and After the Coronation*, depicts the realities of rural life in Northeast China around the time of the "enthronement" of Puyi, the puppet emperor of Manchukuo, between 1932 and 1934. It conveys that, in a time "when the cold night was everywhere," only seeking national liberation is the spark of hope, making its ideological significance quite positive. The author captures one of the darkest and most contradictory periods in the history of Northeast China, giving the work a clear realistic significance. Ma Jia expresses deep sympathy for the tragedy of farmers in Northeast China. The protagonist, Lu Youxiang, suffers in silence after his wife is humiliated by the puppet village chief. The multiple puppet regime's ruthless exploitation of the farmers is vividly portrayed. Ultimately, the anti-Japanese volunteers liberated the village, and Lu Youxiang kills the chief with his own hands before joining the volunteers. These true descriptions possess a compelling force, so vivid that as if they are unfolding before the reader's eyes—something only accessible with firsthand life experience. Additionally, the novel's language carries the distinct flavor of Northeast rural life, rich with country flavor, and its a rigorous and precise structure is particularly outstanding.

While Ma Jia was writing the *Sparks in the Cold Night in Peking*, Xiao Jun and Xiao Hong were completing *Village in August* and *The Field of Life and Death* in Shanghai. These three works are among the earliest and finest to depict the anti-Japanese struggles of the people in Northeast China. They share a consistent theme with excellent description, and all emerged from the pens of young "Northeastern Writers in Exile" However, *Sparks in the Cold Night*, published in Peking, was less widely known at the time, which affected its deserved historical recognition. This oversight should be corrected.

The long poem *Fire Sacrifice* is a lyrical political manifesto poem. The language throughout is as resounding as gold and stone, with a high spirit, like a flame. The rhythm jumps brightly, and the passionate emotions are repeatedly rendered, full of romantic temperament. This poem was rated as the best poem of the year by *The Year Book of China's Art and Culture Industry* in the 1933. In addition, novels such as *Letters from Home*, *The Road of Revenge*, *Hidden Flames*, *Fellow Travelers*, and *The Death of the Old Man* all depict the life in the fallen rural areas of Northeast China, portraying a distorted and decadent society that has become a colony.

Ma Jia's works are deeply rooted in the local flavor of Northeast China, and he is particularly adept at incorporating the everyday language of the people in the region. His writing style is simple, natural, vivid and smooth, and carries a strong regional atmosphere of the Northeast China. Starting with his medium length novel *Ten Days in Jiangshan Village*, Ma Jia consciously pursued a path of nationalized language striving to create a literary language that resonated with the cultural identity of the Chinese people. After the founding of the People's Republic of China, his unique linguistic style matured and became widely praised. It can be said that among Northeast writers, Ma Jia's mastery of Northeast local language stands out as the most exceptional. In his later masterpiece *The Record of the Northern Country* , his linguistic artistry reached a remarkably high level.

Throughout his life, Ma Jia focused on writing about rural life in Northeast China. His works are deeply rooted in the a solid and solid foundation in daily life of the region, reflecting the simple and natural essence of the northern land and its history. The beauty of the Liao River and the fertile black soil of his homeland exude a natural aroma in his writings. Among the "Northeastern Writers in Exile" he, along with Xiao Jun, Luo Feng, Sai Ke, and Bai Lang, belongs to the "Northern School" of writers, whose works are characterized by a robust, simple and natural style. Among the major figures of the "Northeastern Writers in Exile" Ma Jia stands out as the only one who remained in the Northeast after the founding of the People's Republic of China, taking on leadership roles in the cultural front and consistently portraying Northeast life in his works. This unique identity makes him distinctive from his peers.

Chapter 12 Li Huiying: A Beautiful and Simple Homesick Song

Biography

Li Huiying (1911-1991), originally named Li Liancui, pen names Dong Li, Lin Shan, Xi Cun, Bei Ling, Nan Feng, etc, born in Jilin County (now Yongji County), Jilin Province in 1911.

At the age of seven, he enrolled in a private school in his hometown. At the age of thirteen, he was admitted to Jilin Provincial Fifth Middle School and met his picture teacher Zhu Yishi. Zhu Yishi advocated for new ideas and literature, which aroused Li Huiying's strong interest in new literature.

In 1927, Li Huiying graduated from the junior high school of the Jilin Provincial Fifth Middle School. Upon seeing the enrollment advertisement for Lida Academy in *Lida Monthly* published in Shanghai, he resolutely decided to go to Shanghai with 10 classmates and enrolled in the high school department of Lida Academy. *Lida Monthly* was published by the Lida Association, whose members included scholars such as Xia Mianzun, Ye Shengtao, and Zheng Zhenduo. The Association was the predecessor of Kaiming Bookstore and had a significant influence on Chinese intellectuals. At Lida Academy, Li Huiying's horizons broadened. He began to learn how to write novels and co-founded a publication called *Qinglu Journal* with his classmates, showing a progressive ideological tendency. After graduation, he continued his studies at China Public University, where Shen Congwen and Zhao Jingshen once taught.

In September 1931, the outbreak of the Mukden Incident deeply shocked and distressed Li Huiying, who was far away in Shanghai. Filled with indignation, he joined the large anti-Japanese demonstrations in Shanghai and went to Nanjing to petition with patriotic students. He was determined to use his pen as a weapon to express his aspirations and awaken the world, and to resist Japan and save the nation. In his autobiographical account, he stated:

"After the Mukden Incident, Shenyang and Changchun fell, and soon after, a large land in the four provinces of Northeast China was lost and 30 million Chinese people are enslaved. It was in this heartbreaking situation of country perishes that I determined to be a writer" This marked the original intention behind his literary pursuits.

In January 1932, Li Huiying's debut novel, *The Last Lesson*, was published in the first issue of the second volume of *Beidou Journal*, a journal of the Association of Chinese Left-Wing Writers edited by Ding Ling. This was also the first short novel by a "Northeastern Writers in Exile" with the theme of anti-Japanese resistance. In March of the following year, his novel *Wanbao Mountain*, revised and recommended by Ding Ling, was published by Shanghai's Hufeng Bookstore as part of the " A series of books created in the War of Resistance Against Japanese Aggression," alongside *Gears* by Tie Chihan (Zhang Tianyi) and *The Volunteer Army* by Lin Qing (Yang Hansheng). *Wanbao Mountain* was the first full-length novel by a Northeast writer with the theme of anti-Japanese resistance. From then on, this young Northeast writer became active in the literary world with his anti-Japanese-themed works and began corresponding with Lu Xun, whose work, *Lu Xun's Diary*, mentions Li Huiying's name. In 1933, Li Huiying joined the Association of Chinese Left-Wing Writers. In March, he attended a writing symposium organized by the Association, where he listened to Lu Xun's speech. Shortly afterward, he began teaching at Quanzhang Middle School. In 1934, he edited *Chats in Caricature* and *Chuangzuo Monthly* in Shanghai. In the spring of 1936, he moved to Peking, where he collaborated with Sun Xizhen, Cao Jinghua, Wang Xiyan, and others from the Peking Association of Chinese Left-Wing Writers to establish the Peking Writers' Association. He was elected as a member of the first executive committee and served as the editor of its official publication, *Literature Weekly*. During this period, Li Huiying's works and literary activities were dynamic and full of vitality.

In 1932, Li Huiying returned to his hometown in Jilin from Shanghai to gain firsthand life experience. After returning to Shanghai, he wrote several works depicting the hard lives of the people in Northeast China under the enslavement of the Puppet Manchukuo. Following the July 7th Incident in 1937, Li Huiying left Peking and engaged in anti-Japanese Salvation movement in Wuhan, Chongqing, and other places. In 1939, he joined the the Chinese Association of Literary and Art Circles for Resisting Enemy and participated in the Writer's Battlefield Visiting Group organized by the Association. He traveled to the North China frontlines, including the Zhongtiao Mountains, to experience the lives of anti-Japanese soldiers and civilians, producing numerous essays and sketches during this period.

After the victory of the War of Resistance Against Japanese Aggression, Li Huiying returned to Northeast China and served as a professor in the Chinese Department at Changchun University and Northeast University. In 1950, he moved to Hong Kong, where he made a living through writing. Starting in 1963, he taught at the School of Oriental Languages at the University of Hong Kong and later at United College of The Chinese University of Hong Kong. In 1976, he resigned due to illness and returned home to recuperate. In 1984, he traveled from Hong Kong to Beijing to attend the Fourth National Congress of the Chinese Writers' Association, where he was elected as a member of the presidium, once again drawing public attention.

Introduction to Works

Among the "Northeastern Writers in Exile", Li Huiying was one of the earliest to gain attention but was forgotten soon after the founding of the People's Republic of China. He arrived in Shanghai early and had interactions with Lu Xun. His short story *The Last Lesson* and novel *Wanbao Mountain* were among the earliest works by Northeast writers to depict the theme of Northeast people's resistance against Japanese aggression. In his 1936 essay *Literature at the Present*, Zhou Yang remarked: "With the Mukden Incident and the lives and struggles of soldiers, workers, farmers, and urban residents during the Shanghai War as themes, emerging writers such as Zhang Tianyi, Sha Ting, Ai Wu, Li Huiying, Ye Lin, and Ge Qin produced meaningful and fresh works." He Lin, in the *New Literature in the Decade Around the Founding of the Association of Chinese Left-Wing Writers*, noted: "After the Mukden Incident Incident, a group of Northeast writers emerged, including Xiao Jun, Xiao Hong, Shu Qun, Luo Feng, Duanmu Hongliang, Li Huiying, and Hei Ding", which positively affirm Li Huiying's status as a Northeast anti-Japanese writer. After the founding of the People's Republic of China, Li Huiying's name faded from the mainland as he moved to Hong Kong, leading to a gradual sense of unfamiliarity. In fact, Li Huiying was an influential progressive writer during the War of Resistance Against Japanese Aggression. In 1976, during a meeting with Japanese writer Akira Aiura, Li Huiying stated, "My writings carry a strong anti-Japanese consciousness" (as seen in *Remembering Mr. Li Huiying*, published in *Historical Materials of Modern Literature in Northeast China*, Vol. 8). In his later years in Hong Kong, Li Huiying's works frequently expressed deep patriotic and nostalgic sentiments. As an important member of the ""Northeastern Writers in Exile," Li Huiying's status as a progressive anti-Japanese writer should be restored.

Mr. Wang Yao once commented on Li Huiying in the *Northeast Writers Group* in Chapter 8 of the second part of the *The Manuscript of Chinese new Literature History* published by Kaiming Bookstore in 1951. However, when the book was republished by the New Literature and Art Publishing House in 1953, this comment was removed. In order to help readers understand Mr. Wang Yao's description of Li Huiying's position in literary history at that time, the author now transcribes this part as follows:

One of the earlier writers is Li Huiying, whose novel *Wanbao Mountain* attempted to explain the Wanpaoshan Incident before the Mukden Incident as a major movement of Chinese people's anti-Japanese struggle by depicting the years of economic plunder by Japanese imperialism. However, it was not very successful. In 1933, he returned to the Northeast and wrote a short story collection titled *Bountiful Year*. In the preface, the author admonished himself: "You should turn leisurely writing style into a weapon against the enemy! For example, expose the atrocities of Japanese imperialism in the Northeast—oppression, slaughter, and deception of our weak nation. At the same time, you should focus on a certain time of real society and say what needs to be said." This collection represents his attempt to put this into practice. Among the stories, the *Bountiful Year* tells the tale of the Northeast Volunteer Army in the War of Resistance Against Japanese Aggression, depicting how Sun San, a peace-loving old farmer, learned from the facts and lessons that he must participate in the resistance instead of being backward. *The Cobbler* portrays a cobbler in Northeast China who, due to the massive dumping of Japanese rubber shoes that he couldn't repair, spontaneously rebelled against a police who interfered with his stall with anger. Another story, *The Country Folk*, depicts the underground anti-Japanese movement of young students. The themes have practical significance, and the authors also have passionate emotions. The use of Jilin dialect in the works is also well-suited to express the circumstances of the time, which should have made the stories quite outstanding. However, the author's ideology is weak, only superficially presenting phenomena, which diminishes the emotional impact. The writing is fluent but not concise, with too many explanations.

Here, Mr. Wang Yao outlines the general features of Li Huiying's novelistic creations but does not include his essays.

Li Huiying was a diligent writer with a long creative career and a substantial body of work. His major works include the novel *Wanbao Mountain*, *The Trilogy of Resistance Against Japan* comprising *The Foggy*

Capital, *The Human World*, and *The Front*, as well as novels such as *On the Songhua River*, *The Blossom and Fruit of Love*, *Bitter Fruit*, and *Four Sisters*. His medium length novel include *Miss Rose*, *The Pursuit*, *Love in Harbin*, and *Pastoral of the Countryside*. His short story collections include *Two Brothers*, *The Bountiful Year*, *The Human World Collection*, *The Mountains and Rivers Collection*, and *North Collection*. His essay collections include *The Rebirth Collection*, *Between Soldiers and Civilians*, *The Inn in Mountain Valley*, *Travels in China*, *Travels to Famous Chinese Cities*, *Selected Essays of Li Huiying*, *Journey to Singapore and Malaysia*, *Hometown Collection*, and *A Few Words*. Additionally, he wrote dramas, reportage collections, and over a hundred essays that were not compiled into collections.

Li Huiying's primary achievements lie in his novels and essays. His works are characterized by their natural simplicity, fresh elegance, and close connection to real life. Whether in novels or essays, his source material is quite extensive. Some of his works reflect the social realities of Northeast China and reminiscence about his childhood, while others depict the lives of soldiers and civilians on the anti-Japanese front. He also portrays the peculiar and varied social landscape of Shanghai during the War of Resistance Against Japanese Aggression, as well as the customs and scenery of Hong Kong and Southeast Asia. The early works are imbued with his worry about the nation during the war , while the later ones are tinged with nostalgia for his homeland. Over the decades, he never forgot his homeland and Northeast China, his sincere heart of a devoted Chinese remains undiminished, and his poignant patriotic sentiments are touching.

In 1932, Li Huiying published the short story *The Last Lesson*, depicts a female high school student in a provincial city in Northeast China who was insulted by the Japanese army after the the Mukden Incident. Shortly after, he received a letter from Ding Ling asking him, Could you write a full-length novel set in Northeast China to express the theme of anti-Japanese resistance? This suggestion excited him, and he "began collecting materials... and finally completed the work two and a half months later." This marked the origin of the novel *Wanbao Mountain*. This novel is based on the true historical events of the Wanpaoshan Incident in Jilin Province before the Mukden Incident. It portrays how Japanese consuls and Japanese ronin bribed the traitor Hao Yongde, colluded with local officials, and, under the pretext of developing paddy fields, forcibly seized large tracts of fertile land from farmers in the Wanbao Mountain area. This led to conflicts between Chinese and North Korean farmers, ultimately sparking a farmer uprising against the Japanese. The fresh selection of materials, the significance and practicality of the theme make *Wanbao Mountain* a pioneer in the creation of anti Japanese literature in Northeast China.

Due to the author's haste in writing and insufficient life experience, the novel appears rough and is not entirely successful. In the essay *Anti-Japanese Literature After the Mukden Incident: Three Novels*, Mao Dun sharply pointed out the shortcomings of the novel: "The author fails to vividly depict the unique social conditions of 'Northeast China' under the prolonged military control and economic aggression of Japanese imperialism. This is the main flaw of the entire book!" He further criticized, "The novel hardly describes how Japanese imperialist economic aggression led to the irreparable poverty of the Wanbao Mountain farmers. The impression given by the book is that the Wanbao Mountain farmers were originally living a joyful life, when Hao Yongde’s collusion with the Japanese to reclaim wasteland ruined everything, then the farmers began to resist." Mao Dun added, "To write about the social conditions of Northeast China while neglecting the monopolistic control and deep penetration of Japanese imperialist economic forces is a significant error." These are undeniable flaws of the novel. Nevertheless, Mao Dun recognized the positive role the novel played at the time: "Even though these works have shortcomings or even serious errors, the authors' goals are progressive. Readers would be better off reading such works rather than indulging in nauseating romance novels."[1] This is a fair assessment.

Li Huiying's essays are particularly outstanding, characterized by their freshness and natural smooth, making them the most impressive part of his literary work. Everyday trivialities, casually picked up, come to life vividly under his pen. Especially in the author's essays of longing for hometown and reminiscing about childhood life, the naive childlike innocence, the unique scenery of the northern country, and their deep affection for their homeland are portrayed in a simple and unadorned manner, making people yearn for them. In *The Broad Daylight on the Post Road*, he writes: "In the early morning, the sun shines high. It is truly delightful—lush green trees, the silhouette of mountains, and the gentle breeze spreading warmth everywhere, filling me with joy!" This reflects the author's joyful mood upon returning to his hometown. *The Hometown Collection*, written in Hong Kong, is one of Li Huiying's most touching series of essays. Like a string of exquisite pearls or a series of northern folk art paintings, they entice readers to appreciate the majestic beauty of the north, with a writing style that is exceptionally simple and elegant. *Nostalgia for My Hometown* expresses the author's sincere longing for his childhood home, Jinjiatun when he grew up, exuding a refreshing atmosphere. Some of its most beautiful passages can rival the *Eepilogue* of Xiao Hong's *Tales of Hulan River*. Essays like *Ice, Snow, Deep Winter and Severe Cold* and *Memories of Snow* depict the scenes of Northeast China during the frozen season with heavy snow. Farmers, wearing thick straw boots, drive sleds across the snow, while children use bird traps to catch sparrows on the snow, filled with childlike innocence. The atmosphere of these works is joyful. Additionally, in essays such as *Soil and Rusticity*, *Country Children*, *The Cart*, *Grazing on the Pasture*, *Celebrating the New Year*, and *Mountain Village*, the author portrays the constant busyness and hopes of

---

1 *Dongfangweiming: Anti-Japanese Literature After the Mukden Incident: Three Novels, Literature*, Volume 1, Issue 2, 1933.

farmers through the eyes of a child. The sight of big grain trucks with firecrackers, the calls of peddlers moving from village to village, the high stacks of firewood piled in front of each house, and the frozen water vats—all these scenes come alive before the reader's eyes, vividly capturing the authentic winter scenery of Northeast China's countryside. When the author recalls stealing cucumbers with his childhood friends, the mischievous country children sing songs like "Flat pole hook, drift with the water" or "Sickle handle, don't be afraid" to report the stealing, filling with a lively atmosphere. This joyful tone is a unique technique used by Li Huiying to describe her hometown in Northeast China, and is rare among other northeastern writers. Due to Japanese aggression, these joyful things were lost and only exist in his memory. Because they cannot be forgotten, the impressions are even deeper. When this joyful atmosphere contrasts sharply with the oppression of leaving his homeland, it naturally evokes an indescribable sense of melancholy and sorrow in the author's heart. Observant readers will surely take notice of the underlying poignant and lingering emotions.

Li Huiying's creative personality combines the strengths of both southern and northern literary traditions, which may be related to his life experiences. The realistic spirit, local flavor, and unadorned writing style of his works leave a deep impression on readers. As a writer from Northeast China, his name will forever be remembered by the people of the Northeast.

Chapter 13 Mu Mutian and Gao Lan: People Always Remember Their Songs

Biography

Mu Mutian (1900–1971), originally named Mu Jingxi, was born on March 26, 1900, in Yitong, Jilin Province. He began his education at a private school at the age of 6. In 1914, he enrolled at Jilin Provincial Middle School, and in 1915, he transferred to Nankai Middle School in Tianjin. After graduating from middle school in 1918, he went to Japan for further studies, where he once took a group photo with Zhou Enlai and other Nankai alumni in Atami, Japan. Mu Mutian had a strong interest in chemistry and mathematics and once dreamed of saving the nation through science. However, influenced by the May Fourth Movement and his poor vision, he shifted his focus to literature. In 1920, he studied the liberal arts program at the Third High School in Kyoto, Japan. He began his literary activities in 1921 and joined the Society of Creation. In 1923, he enrolled in the French Literature Department at the University of Tokyo, where he was deeply influenced by French Symbolism. After graduating from the University of Tokyo in 1926, he published his first poetry collection, *Traveling Heart*, which expressed a tone of melancholy and sorrow. In the summer of the same year, he returned to China and taught at Sun Yat-sen University in Guangzhou, where he married Mai Daoguang. However, due to differences in interests, hobbies, and emotions, they later divorced. At the end of the year, he moved to Beijing and Tianjin to teach. In 1927, he returned to Jilin and taught at the provincial university. In early 1931, he moved to Shanghai and joined the Association of Chinese Left-Wing Writers. In 1932, he joined the Communist Party of China (he left the party after being arrested in 1934) and married Peng Hui. In September of that year, together with Yang Sao, Pu Feng, Ren Jun, and others, he co-founded the China Poem Party in Shanghai. In February of the following year, he launched the *New Poetry*, a periodical appearing once every ten days. In it, he criticized the poetic styles of aestheticism and formalism, calling on poets to "focus on reality and commend the consciousness of the new era," to make poetry "the songs of the masses," and to advocate for the "folklorization of new poetry." He also completed his second poetry collection, *The Songs of the Exiles*.

After the fall of Shanghai in 1937, Mu Mutian returned to Wuhan, where he served as the editor of the poetry journals *Melody of the Times* and *Wuyue*. He was also appointed as a council member of the Chinese Association of Literary and Art Circles for Resisting Enemy and organized poetry recitation activities. In 1938, he moved to Kunming, where he became a standing council member of the Yunnan branch of the Chinese Association of Literary and Art Circles for Resisting Enemy. In 1940, he began teaching at Sun Yat-sen University. By 1942, he went to Guilin, where, in addition to teaching at Guilin Normal College, he translated works by the French author Honoré de Balzac and published his poetry collection *A New Journey*. In 1947, he moved to Shanghai to teach at Tongji University.

After the founding of the People's Republic of China, Mu Mutian returned to teach at Northeast Normal University in Changchun in 1949. In 1952, he was transferred to the Chinese Department of Beijing Normal University as a professor and director of the Foreign Literature Teaching and Research Office. Since then, he has been busy with teaching and has not written much poetry. In 1957, he was wrongly classified as a rightist. During the Cultural Revolution, he was criticized for his mistakes and passed away in October 1971. After the downfall of the Gang of Four, under the care of the Central Organization Department, Mu Mutian and Peng Hui were able to be exonerated. On November 17, 1981, a memorial service for Mu Mutian was held at the Babaoshan Revolutionary Cemetery. In the eulogy, Mu Mutian was described as an influential poet and advocate of the revolutionary poetry movement in the history of new literature since the May Fourth Movement, a renowned translator and researcher of foreign literature, and a passionate educator.

Gaolan (1909-1987), originally named Guo Dehao, used pen names such as Heisha, Guo Hao, Hao, Qi Yun, etc. Born on October 11th, 1909 in Aihui, Heilongjiang Province. He lost his father at the age of 3, and his mother was from the Daur ethnic group.

In 1921, he enrolled in the First Normal School of Heilongjiang Province. After graduation, he enrolled in the second year of the liberal arts at Beijing Chongshi High School, and transferred to the third year of Beijing Huiwen High School the following year. From 1928 to 1932, he studied at the Chinese Department of Yanjing University. Coinciding with the Mukden Incident, he deeply felt the tragic disaster of national destruction and family loss, actively engaged in progressive literary creation, and participated in the student petition activity for the southward movement.

After the July 7th Incident in 1937, he moved to Shanghai and then went to Wuhan, dedicating himself to the creation of recitation poetry. His poem *Our Memorial Ceremony* was recited at the memorial meeting in Wuhan as a tribute to the first anniversary of Mr. Lu Xun's death and was also published in *Combat*, receiving significant attention. Many of his recitation poems were broadcast on radio stations in Hankou and Chongqing, such as *My Home is in Heilongjiang* and *The Cry of the Lost Daughter Sophie* which circulated among the people during the War of Resistance Against Japanese Aggression. By the end of 1937, his poetry collection *Gao Lan's Recitation Poems* was published and well-received. In 1943, *A New Collection of Gao Lan's Recitation Poems* was also published. His recitation poems during the war played a significant role in promoting the colloquial, combative, and popular aspects of poetry, praised by Mao Dun as "the re-liberation movement of new poetry." After the founding of the People's Republic of China, he wrote *My Life is Good* which was also widely recited by people.

In 1947, Gao Lan served as the editor of the literary weekly at the *Northeast People's Daily* in Shenyang. The following year, he became a part-time professor in the Chinese Department of Changchun University. Then he served as a professor at Shandong Normal University and Jinan East China University. In 1951, he joined the China Democratic League and was appointed as a professor in the Chinese Department of Shandong University in the same year. After that, he primarily focused on theoretical research and teaching in poetry. Gao Lan passed away due to illness on June 29, 1987.

Introduction to Works

Mu Mutian was the most senior poet among the Northeastern Writers in Exile and one of the most accomplished poets of the later period of the Society of Creation, as noted by Wang Yao in his *The Manuscript of Chinese new Literature History*. His contributions are primarily reflected in his new poetry and translations of progressive foreign literature.

Mu Mutian published three poetry collections: *Traveling Heart*, *The Song of the Exiles*, and *A New Journey*. These collections collectively reflect his ideological and artistic achievements across three different periods.

The Traveling Heart was written during the author's study abroad in Japan from 1923 to 1926. Its tone is melancholic, belonging to the pastoral and love poetry genre, with an emphasis on artistic refinement. Heavily influenced by French modernist poetry, its content is relatively insubstantial. By contrast, *The Song of the Exiles*, written between 1930 and 1936, marked a dramatic shift in his poetic style. From 1929 to 1931, the poet returned to Jilin, just before the Mukden Incident. Witnessing the arrogance of the Japanese invaders, the decline of Northeast China's rural areas, the rampant corruption ("gentry and bandits everywhere," "opium and morphine everywhere"), he deeply felt the "chains" weighing on the people and the "burdens they carried." He declared: "I always longed, like Du Fu reflecting the social realities of the Tang Dynasty, to cry out in poetry the hardships endured by the people of the Northeast in recent years." Because of the changes in his thoughts and emotions, his creations are more consciously reflecting the times, so the poetic style has changed from delicate to strong, and his focus has shifted from the ivory tower to the middle of ordinary people's lives In his poems, he exposed the dangers of Japanese aggression in the Northeast China and passionately voiced the suffering of his compatriots. The fate of the nation and its people, their sorrow and struggle, became the new themes of his poetry. He lamented: "Since my final farewell to the Northeast China, the sorrow of longing for my homeland has constantly welled up in my heart." Notable poems from this collection—such as *To the Young Friends of the Northeast*, *Here Comes the Grayish-white Dawn Again*, *At Fengtian Station*, *Night in a Riverside Village*, and *On the Harabaling Mountains*—are imbued with patriotic fervor and concern for the people, representing the best of this period. For example, these lines from *At Fengtian Station*: "Countless bayonets pierce the people's flesh, countless bayonets stab into the people's hearts, but one day, when the people awaken to their pain, they will raise the flag and rebel against you at that time." Or from *On the Harabaling Mountains*:

Now, in the night, upon the ancient, somber woods,
Only the weight of dark clouds presses down,
And the howling echoes through the valleys like ghosts and wolves—
Yet scarcely a single traveler can be seen.
Though Japanese sentries patrol the road,
Lurking in threes and fives, guarding the newly laid railway,
Their faint lanterns, their shifting shadows,
Only deepen the gloom, the suffocating darkness.

These lengthy, solemn lines gives off a powerful feeling, showcasing a robust realist poetic style that marks this as one of Mu Mutian's most prominent works.

Mu Mutian's third poetry collection, *A New Journey*, compiles poems written between 1937 and 1940. Amid the fervor of the War of Resistance Against Japanese Aggression, the poet's impassioned spirit became even more pronounced—his style grew more resolute, his emotions more vigorous and unyielding, pulsating with impassioned cries of resistance. Consciously refining his craft, Mu Mutian sought to make his poetry more fluid and accessible to the masses. He ardently championed "realistic lyrical poetry" meant for recitation poems, calling for poems to "become the songs of the masses, and ourselves to merge into them." In the rising tide of wartime poetry, Mu Mutian stood as an exemplary practitioner. After the August 13th Incident in Shanghai, he wrote *The Total Mobilization of the Nation*:

The earth shall henceforth roar with the fury of the oppressed!
Now is the time to reclaim the Northeast, to storm the bandits' lair!
Rage on, China— now is the time!

Simple, direct, and nearly colloquial, the poem is consisted of calls and fury, perfectly suited to the tumultuous era. Similarly, a stanza from *To Hui* strikes an even crisper, more resolute tone:

Hui! Tell Lili to shout aloud:
'Papa, give me an extra bowl of rice—
I'll go fight the Japanese devils alone if I must!'

This poem, both in form and spirit, epitomizes the essence of Mu Mutian's poetry during this period. His poems often feature long, powerful lines, layered with parallelism and strong political undertones, lending them a stirring, inspiring quality. Mu Mutian also placed great emphasis on poetic form and the popular style. He once remarked: "The New Poetry Movement has been underway for fifteen or sixteen years, and while it has made some works, it has yet to reach the broader populace. Remaining confined to a minority and failing to attain mass appeal must, in some sense, be considered a failure." (Mu Mutian, *On the Creation of Folk Ballads*). He pays attention to the mass, resistance, and reality of poetry, and recognizes the significance of poetry resonating with the times. In doing so, he carried forward the distinguished realist tradition of Chinese poetry. Precisely because he not only vigorously advocated these principles but also embodied them in practice, he was hailed by Li Huiying as "the foremost figure in poetic achievement among the 'Northeastern Writers in Exile[1]".

Mu Mutian left behind a considerable body of poems, but few are considered refined masterpieces. This was largely because, while advocating for the popularization of poetry and its service to the resistance, he often neglected the artistic refinement of his poems. His lines were straightforward, impassioned, and inspiring—effective in boosting morale but overly explicit and prioritizes momentum over depth of imagery. Nevertheless, his work remains a testament to the indelible historical contributions of Northeastern anti Japanese writers. Beyond poetry, Mu Mutian also achieved remarkable distinction as a renowned translator of foreign literature and an influential educator.

Gao Lan emerged as another influential poet among the "Northeastern Writers in Exile" and a pioneer of Anti-Japanese recitation poetry. He emerged from the snowstorm in the northern border and joined the ranks of anti Japanese writers in Northeast China with his strong Northeastern regional color and anti Japanese sentiment in his poems.

His most renowned work, *My Home is in Heilongjiang*:

Only by Qingming Festival does the river thaw—

[1] Li Huiying: *A Few Incidents in the Literary World of the Early 1930s*, *Changqing*, November 1980

Great blocks of ice,
Jade-like beds,
Marble sculptures adrift,
Ceaselessly flowing day and night,
Ceaselessly roaring day and night:
A mighty hymn to spring beyond the Great Wall.
Come October, snowflakes large as palms
Bury our embroidered rivers and mountains
Under boundless white.
Jade trees and silver blossoms everywhere—
No more cottages, no more fields.
Wayfarers on the road
Resemble lone crows vanishing into clouds!

Among his contemporaries, Gao Lan stands unparalleled in depicting the majestic grandeur of the North through this poem. His writing is unadorned yet exquisite, sincere and moving. The drifting river ice-the "jade-like beds," and the snow-blanketed villages decorated by “jade trees and silver blossoms”depicts the majestic spirit and natural beauty of the North. Particularly unforgettable is the line: "Resemble lone crows vanishing into clouds." This haunting image has become iconic, sparking endless interpretations—a testament to Gao Lan's genius. Only one who loves his homeland with unwavering devotion could craft such poignant verse. Here, patriotism and homesickness merge seamlessly, each reinforcing the other in a powerful emotional alloy.

During the wartime mobilization in Wuhan, Gao Lan's recitation poetry became a powerful propaganda weapon, electrifying crowds with its visceral urgency. His iconic poem *It's Time, My Compatriots*:

Men roar,

Horses neigh,
The heavens spin,
The earth quakes—
Bullets leap in rifle chambers,
Broadswords howl in gripped hands!
Charge!
Charge!
Blood debts are paid in blood alone.
Shall we show mercy to invaders?

The poem's momentum is unbroken and forceful, its rhythm sharp and distinct, its language terse and resonant, brimming with fervent patriotic passion and an uplifting tone. Other works like *Nine Years*, *Our Memorial Rite*, *The Cry of the Lost Daughter Sophie*, *On the Hilltop*, and *The Homeland's Sky Bursts into Bloom* were also widely recited among the masses at the time. Pulsing with the heartbeat of the era, these poems channeled the people's heartfelt emotions as they joined the torrent of resistance, leaving a profound impact.

For example, in the *Goodbye*, Miss, the author calls on young people to join the War of Resistance Against Japanese Aggression, and the enthusiastic tone has a great appeal:

Why in tears, my dearest one?
Who among us hasn't lain in a mother's arms counting stars?
Who hasn't disturbed weeping willows in a lover's embrace?
But now—our nation in ruins, our homes destroyed!
We who grovel as slaves in hell,
How dare we cling to dreams of paradise?

Gao Lan's poetry is characterized by its overflowing patriotic fervor, colloquial clarity, and the organic eruption of zeitgeist from personal conviction. His works exhibit both majestic grandeur and delicate brilliance. He pioneered the use of modern poetic forms to depict the landscapes of his homeland Heilongjiang, becoming the first Northeastern writer to do so with such distinction. However, after the victory of the War of Resistance Against Japanese Aggression, his poetry gradually drifted apart from the surging currents of the new era. Following the establishment of the People's Republic of China, he devoted himself primarily to teaching, producing few new works—an undoubted loss to Chinese poems.

Chapter 14 Sai Ke: A Pioneer of Anti-Japanese Drama

Biography

Sai Ke (1906–1988), originally named Chen Ningqiu, was born on July 26, 1906 into a farmer family in Baxian County, Hebei Province (now Bazhou City). After completing primary school at hometown, he left for Harbin in 1922. In 1924, he became an editor and editor-in-chief of the literary supplement of Harbin's *Chenguang Daily*. Due to his radical ideology and revolutionary behaviors, he was arrested and imprisoned in 1926. After three month's imprisonment, he subsequently lost his job.

In August 1927, Sai Ke went to Shanghai and enrolled at Shanghai Art University to study fine arts and literature. He gained recognition for his lead role in the Japanese play *The Father's Return*, performed by the "Fish and Dragon Society" (the "Southern China Society" predecessor), marking the beginning of his involvement in dramas. He later played leading roles in progressive dramas such as *Return to the South* and *Salome*, which further established his fame. In 1928, he published his first poetry collection, *The Pursuit*.

In 1929, Sai Ke returned to Harbin. Deeply drawn to the Soviet Union, he once traveled to Manzhouli but was unable to cross the border due to a lack of a passport. Back in Harbin, he published his second poetry collection, *Songs of Purple*. In 1930, he wrote, directed, and starred in the play *Return to the North*; in 1931, he directed the drama *Harbin Night*, performed at a charity event for disaster relief in Harbin. After the Mukden Incident, with the help of underground Communist Party members Jin Jianxiao and Jiang Chunfang, Sai Ke boarded a refugee train to Suifen River in early winter 1931 and entered Soviet Union through Dongning. However, Soviet Union's border guards suspected him of espionage and detained him in Khabarovsk for an entire winter. He was repatriated to Suifen River in the spring of 1932. Disillusioned, he begged his way to Xiaosuifen River and, in frustration, joined an anti-Japanese volunteer army. Six months later, the force disbanded on its own. In the spring of 1933, he returned to Shanghai once again.

In Shanghai, at the invitation of Hong Shen, Sai Ke entered the film industry. He played leading roles in movies such as *Tears on Iron Plate*, *Common Enemy*, *Shanghai's 24 Hours*, and *The Romance of Huashan Mountain*. In 1934, he used the pen name "Sai Ke" for the first time to write the famous anti-Japanese drama *Thirty Million Refugees*, with its theme song composed by Xian Xinghai. This marked their collaboration on China's first renowned anti-Japanese salvation song. The drama premiered successfully at the Shanghai Grand Theater in 1935. Afterward, Sai Ke wrote other dramas, including *The Iron Squad*, *The Prison,* and *The Taiping Heavenly Kingdom*, as well as famous poems like *The National Salvation Army Song* and *Hatred in the Heart*. He also translated Maxim Gorky's *The Lower Depths* and the lyrics of many Soviet songs, remaining highly active in both literary creation and theatrical performances.

Following the outbreak of the War of Resistance Against Japanese Aggression in Shanghai in 1937, Sai Ke wrote dramas such as *Defend the Marco Polo Bridge* and *The National War of Resistance Against Japan*. He served as a council member of the China Anti-Japanese Association of Drama Players and joined the First Team of Shanghai Salvation Performance Troupe, traveling to Nanjing, Henan, Shanxi, and other regions to stage anti-Japanese propaganda performances. In October 1938, he joined the Northwest Battlefield Service Groups, led by Ding Ling, in Linfen, where he collaborated with Xian Xinghai to compose *The Song of the Northeast National Salvation Association*. After co-writing the drama *The Raid*, he arrived in Yan'an.

In Yan'an, Sai Ke served as the director of the Yan'an Youth Theater and vice-chairman of the Border Region Branch of China Anti-Japanese Association of Drama Players. He directed dramas such as *The Armored Train* and worked with Xian Xinghai to create *The Great Chorus of Production*, which achieved great success. In 1939, Yan'an's Luxun Academy of Fine Arts staged his drama *Thirty Million Refugees*, with Xian Xinghai composing an additional interlude, *March of the Manchurian Prisoners*, which garnered significant acclaim. In 1941, Sai Ke was elected as a council member of the Shaanxi-Gansu-Ningxia Border Region Government and a member of the Border Region Cultural Committee. He participated in the Yan'an Forum on Literature and Art in 1942 and enrolled at the Central Party School in 1943. During this period, he wrote the drama *Annihilation* and several anti-Japanese songs.

After the victory of the War of Resistance Against Japanese Aggression, Sai Ke held several key positions in Northeast China, including director of the Federation of Literary and Art Circles of Rehe Province and Jiamusi, standing committee member of the Northeast Federation of Literary and Art Circles, director of the Northeast Drama Committee, president of the Northeast Luxun Academy of Fine Arts, and deputy director of the Education Department of Liaobei Province concurrently serving as vice president of Liaobei College. In 1949, he attended the First National Literature and Arts Congress and was elected as a standing committee member of the National Federation of Literary and Art Circles and a council member of the Chinese Dramatists Association. In 1951, he became the president of the Northeast People's Art Theatre. In 1953, he served as an advisor to the Central Experimental Opera House, which later became the China National Opera and Dance Drama Theater.

In 1956, to commemorate the completion of the Monument to the People's Heroes, Sai Ke published the long poem *The Monument*.

On November 18, 1988, Sai Ke passed away in Beijing.

Introduction to Works

Sai Ke was a multi-talented figure among the "Northeastern Writers in Exile." He worked as a drama actor, film actor, and director, while also distinguishing himself as a novelist, dramatist, and poet. He wrote novels depicting life in Northeast China and published several poetry collections, but his most outstanding contributions were his anti-Japanese dramas. Of the more than 10 scripts he wrote, 9 were composed during the war, directly addressing the theme of resistance and national salvation. Among them, *Thirty Million Refugees*, *Defend the Marco Polo Bridge*, *The Raid*, and *Eight Hundred Heroes* gained the greatest renown.

The Thirty Million Refugees stands as Sai Ke's masterpiece. This three-act play was originally published in the third issue of the *Literature Collections* in June 1936. It was the first script by a "Northeastern Writers in Exile" published inside Shanhaiguan to depict the lives of compatriots in Northeast China under Japanese puppet rule.

The drama depicts Northeast China after its fall to the enemy—a living hell where Japanese invaders left behind a trail of burning, killing, looting, and broken families. The Japanese frenziedly captured laborers, imposed poll taxes, arrested "thought criminals," and forced prisoners to build airfields and mine ore. The protagonist, Zhou Keming, is one such "prisoner." As a resolute anti-Japanese intellectual, he attempts to escape with the help of fellow inmates by breaking his shackles but is discovered by the enemy and ultimately buried alive. As Zhou Keming is forced step by step toward the pit, the prisoners are compelled to shovel dirt onto him until only his head remains above ground. When they can no longer bear to continue, a Japanese soldier grins hideously and kicks Zhou's face with his boot—a scene of unbearable tragedy. Yet Zhou Keming is not alone in his suffering; his strangled life and spilled blood symbolize the fate of thirty million compatriots in China. Covered in blood, the people step over the bodies of their compatriots and the ruins of their homes. As they sing and shout in defiance, the drama's theme song surges forth like a storm, striking deep into the hearts of the audience:

Crimson blood against a blazing sun,
A surging force, a vengeful will aflame,
We are exiles from the Black River's shores,
We are survivors of the iron prison's flame.

The iron hooves of tyranny crush land and stream,
Imperial guns aim at the starving throng.
The sky is torn by hands of wicked might,
The winds howl blood, the heavens scream with wrong.

Our scarred hearts bear the brand of purple pain,
Yet clenched within our teeth is hate untold.
With final resolve, we rise again,
To cleanse our land, our sacred Chinese soil,
And carve a path where slaves may break their chain.

How profoundly tragic and stirring these lyrics are—like lightning splitting the night sky, like a rooster heralding the dawn. They invigorated those fighting in the war and comforted those in exile. The *Thirty Million Refugees* moved audiences with its grand theme of the era, its raw portrayal of life in Northeast China, and its soul-shaking artistic power. The unyielding will of the enslaved it depicted was precisely what that turbulent age demanded. Audience had no time to dwell on the drama's structural disorder and roughness; instead, they were overwhelmed by its visceral indictment, a thunderous cry of "blood and fury."

Sai Ke also collaborated with Xian Xinghai to create *The National Salvation Army Song*, which spread widely among anti-Japanese masses:

Muzzles outward, march in stride!

Harm no civilians! Strike not our own!
We are an iron force, with hearts of steel,
Guarding the Chinese nation, forever free!"

Additionally, *The Song of the Northeast National Salvation Association* and *The Great Chorus of Production*, both with lyrics by Sai Ke, were immensely popular. *The Great Chorus of Production*, reflecting life in the liberated areas during the war, remained a long-standing favorite:

February brings spring's fair light,
Every household toils in fields with might.
Praying for a harvest rich this year,
To fill the army's grain-chest dear.

Sai Ke possessed not only artistic talent but also a keen artistic sensitivity, which gave his work extraordinary appeal when combined with the surging tides of his era. He consistently immersed himself among the masses and had a remarkable ability to articulate his lived experiences. His works—imbued with a powerful zeitgeist, a plain yet vibrant style, and accessible, fluid forms—resonated deeply with the public.

His novel *The East Road Line* depicts the anti-Japanese resistance of people in the Mudanjiang region of Northeast China after the Mukden Incident. While the novel may show some artistic immaturity, it brims with the spirit of the times and remains a compelling read. Additionally, his two early poetry collections, *The Pursuit* and *Songs of Purple*, reflect his personal struggles and quest for meaning in society. Sai Ke's multifaceted artistic achievements are a source of pride for the people of Northeast China.

Chapter 15 Other Northeastern Writers

Jin Ren（1910—1971）

Jin Ren, originally named Zhang Junti and Zhang Shaoyan, also used pen names such as Tian Feng and Zhang Kainian. He was born in Nangong, Hebei Province.

In 1927, Jin Ren went to Harbin to work as an employee at the Eastern Provincial Special District Local Court. In 1928, he became an editor at *Greater North New Daily*. By 1930, he returned to the Court as a trainee Russian translator while studying law. During this time, he began engaging in literary writing. After the Mukden Incident, he wrote essays, novels, and poems opposing Japanese aggression. In 1933, he met and had close exchanges with Luo Feng, Jin Jianxiao, Jiang Chunfang, Shu Qun, Xiao Jun, Xiao Hong and others. Starting in 1934, he dedicated himself to translating Soviet literature. His translations, such as *The Sorrows of Young Werther* and *The Abdication*, were published in *Translation*, a magazine edited by Lu Xun. He also contributed novels, poems, and critical essays to the *International Association News* in Harbin and the supplement of *Min Bao* in Heilongjiang. His works included: poems: *The Wounded Soul*, *Remembering Someone*, *The Past*, and *The Triumph of Death*; essays: *Childishness*, *The Morality of Philanthropists*, *Leisure and Wealth*, and *Nonsense*; novels: *The Way Out*, *Destiny*, and *Repentance*.

In early 1937, Jin Ren left Harbin for Shanghai, embarking on a new phase of his career focused primarily on translating progressive foreign literature. His earliest translations were recommended by Lu Xun. At the beginning of 1935, Jin Ren had just completed his translation of the Soviet work *Funny Stories* and sent it to Xiao Jun. Xiao Jun then wrote to Lu Xun, who expressed his willingness to assist. After reading Jin Ren's work, Lu Xun was quite impressed and wrote to Xiao Jun, saying, "I've read Jin Ren's translation—his writing is remarkably good." He also encouraged Jin Ren to translate more and faster, adding, "There shouldn't be any issues with censorship, and sales will likely be decent. Why not invite him to translate more and include his works in the series?" His words were filled with unmistakable warmth and support. Later, *Funny Stories* was finally published.

In 1942, Jin Ren went to the liberated areas of northern Jiangsu and served as the director of the Judicial Department of the Northern Jiangsu Administrative Office. In 1943, he returned to Shanghai under the guise of a lawyer to engage in underground work. In 1945, he returned to northern Jiangsu and served as the director of the Legal Affairs Committee of the Central Jiangsu Administrative Committee.

During the War of Resistance Against Japan, Jin Ren translated the famous novel *The Quiet Don River* by Soviet writer Sholokhov. Later, he translated works such as *Ivan Nigulin - Russian Sailor*, *Military Diary*, and *City in the Desert*, making contributions to Chinese readers' early understanding of excellent works of Soviet literature.

After the victory of the War of Resistance Against Japanese Aggression, in 1946, Jin Ren went to work at the Chinese Association of Literary and Art Circles for Resisting Enemy in Northeast China. Later, he moved to Harbin, serving as deputy director of the Research Department and Director of the Publishing Department of the Association. In 1948, he was appointed director of the secretariat of the Judicial Department of the Northeast Administrative Committee. In November 1949, he became deputy director of the Compilation and Translation Bureau of the General Administration of Press and Publication. In 1951, he worked as a translator and editor at Shidai Publishing House and later at People's Literature Publishing House. During the War to Resist US Aggression and Aid Korea, he co-translated *Private Aleksandr Matrosov*.

Jin Ren has achievements in translation and writing, and after the founding of the People's Republic of China, he also published many essays and comments, such as *I Love My Motherland*, *Spring Comes to Beijing*, *Talking about the Film 'Quiet Don River' Part 1*, etc. He translated the famous Soviet writer Panfilov's novel *The Grindstone Farm* and Kochetov's *The Zhurbin Family*, and in 1959, he retranslated *The Quiet Don River*. In addition, there are translated works such as *The City on the Grassland* and *The World in the South* by Suilafimovich, *The Grassland* by Chekhov, and *Just Love* by Vasilyevskaya, B. Sobko's *The True Face of the Allies*, Gorky's *The Life of Krim Samkin*, Nikolai Vercingnikov's *Lenin's Childhood*, and Fadeyev's *Young Guards*.

After the founding of the People's Republic of China, Jin Ren became a famous foreign literary translator in China. During the Cultural Revolution, he was persecuted and died in 1971 at the Danjiangkou branch of the Ministry of Culture's 57th Cadre School, at the age of only 61. After the downfall of the Gang of Four, he was rehabilitated.

Lin Jue（1914-1971）

Lin Jue, originally named Tang Jingyang, used pen names such as Da Qiu, Jingyang, Jing Yang, and Liu Er. He was born in Anda, Heilongjiang Province.

In 1929, Lin Jue arrived in Harbin, where he first apprenticed at Tongji Factory and later studied at the Second Middle School. During his school years, he held progressive ideals and actively participated in literary activities. In 1933, he joined the Anti-Japanese Society led by the Communist Party of China in Harbin. During this period, he published numerous short stories, poems, and other works in the supplements of Harbin's *International Association Newspaper*, *Greater North New Daily*, *Harbin Five-Day Pictorial*, and Changchun's *Da Tong Daily*. His works included *Scattered Fragments*, *Night*, *In Anguish*, *The Cry*, *Numbness*, *Return*, *Autumn Night*, *Rural Poems*,

Farewell to the Exiles, *The Dissolute Chairman*, and over fifty others, with poetry being the majority. His writings expressed indignation toward the dark realities of society, sympathy for the laboring people, and his own inner turmoil and aspirations. He maintained connections with writers such as Xiao Jun and Shu Qun.

In September 1936, Lin Jue and his wife Zhou Yulan left Harbin for Shanghai, where he actively engaged in anti-Japanese literary activities. In 1939, his short story collection *The Mountain Village* was published by Shanghai Culture and Life Publishing House. Lin Jue joined the Communist Party of China in Shanghai in 1938. In February 1941, following an assignment by the Party, he went to the anti-Japanese base in northern Jiangsu and joined the New Fourth Army. He worked successively at the Lu Xun Literature and Art University, the Political Department of the New Fourth Army's Third Division, the Northern Jiangsu United Middle School, and the Northern Jiangsu Construction Technical School. In November 1945, he returned to Harbin and served as the president of *Harbin Daily* and deputy president of *Northeast Daily*. Later, he held several key positions, including secretary general of the Harbin Municipal People's Government, director of the Education Bureau, deputy director of the Propaganda Department of the Harbin Municipal Committee of the CPC, deputy director of the Cultural and Educational Committee of the Songjiang Provincial People's Government, director of the Education Department, vice president of Shenyang Normal College, and in 1958, vice president of Liaoning University. During the Cultural Revolution, he and his wife Zhou Yulan were persecuted to death. Then they were officially rehabilitated in December 1977.

Lin Jue's literary achievements primarily lie in his short stories, particularly represented by his three collections: *The Mountain Village*, *Under the Lash*, and *The Kindling*.

The Mountain Village was written shortly after Lin Jue arrived in Shanghai. This collection includes five works that expose the realities of the society in Northeast China under the rule of Japanese-puppet regime. Among them, *The Hoe* depicts the savage brutality of the Japanese invaders by describing how they publicly executed four so-called "criminals" with a hoe in the street. *The Mountain Village* portrays Japanese invaders force forcibly relocating an entire village's population to a so-called "pacified zone" a hundred miles away which sparks resistance among the farmers. The story reflects a progressive ideological stance, highlighting the people's defiance against oppression.

Under the Lash and Kindling were written slightly later. The first part of Under the Lash depicts life in Shanghai during the early stages of the War of Resistance Against Japanese Aggression, with particularly notable stories including *The Old Man* and *Dawn Chronicle. The Old Man* portrays an elderly farmer who braves Japanese artillery fire to deliver food to anti-Japanese soldiers at the front. Pleading with the company commander to let him stay—"Let me charge with you", "Let this old bone be of some use"—he is eventually wounded but declares with satisfaction: "At least I died a glorious death." Though with just over two thousand words, the story is a sharply focused sketch. Through the old man's distinctive actions and dialogue, it vividly captures the Chinese people's fervent desire to resist the invaders. *Dawn Chronicle* presents a microcosm of occupied Shanghai: the destitute sleep on the streets, huddled under rags for warmth, while across the road, foreign sailors and courtesans revel all night in dance halls. On the Huangpu River, "beast-like gunboats" cast covetous eyes on the city. These microcosms ruthlessly expose the grotesque decay of Shanghai under occupation.

Parts Two and *Three of Under the Lash* shift their focus to life in Northeast China occupied by Japanese invaders. Compared to The Mountain Village, these sections demonstrate a more progressive ideological stance, with sharper and more visceral depictions that immerse readers in the harsh realities of the time. Stories like *A Visitor's Account* and *Voice from the Hometown* expose the truth of colonial oppression through the dictations of Northeastern refugees in Shanghai. Schools at all levels enforced assimilationist policies—students were forced to speak Japanese and wear "serge uniforms identical to those of Japanese students." Boys underwent military drills while girls stitched "comfort bags," washed clothes for "garrison headquarters," and even "practiced infant care"... Conscription was rampant. One desperate couple, to spare their only son from service, had the mother rub tobacco dust into his eyes until they bled. Though he was deemed unfit for service, the boy suffered months of agony and "ultimately lost sight in one eye."... Lin Jue recounts these harrowing details with a calm and composed attitude, allowing millions of readers to understand and feel the real suffering of the people in Northeast China at that time. His narratives—whether *The Detainee*, *Under the Lash*, *Selling the Farmland*, *Year's End*, or *The Unyielding Child*—blend stirring defiance with profound introspection, all executed with masterful technique.

Lin Jue's short stories on anti-Japanese themes are exceptional. Compact yet powerful, they possess a strong sense of historical authenticity and social realism. His words flows with understated emotion, achieving remarkable ideological depth and artistic sophistication that placed them among the finest works of his time—a rare accomplishment indeed.

Kong Luosun（1912—1996）

Kong Luosun originally came from Shanghai and was born in Jinan, Shandong Province. He used pen names such as Luo Sun, Lu Sun, Meng Sihuan, Ye Zhiqiu, Ye Li, Yu Wen Zhou, Dong Dai, Luo Yihan, and Zhou Mi.

Kong Luosun completed his primary and secondary education in Shanghai and Beijing. In 1928, his family relocated to Harbin, where he secured employment at the city's post and telecommunications office, working as a staff at the post office in Daowai Wudao Street. It was during this period that he developed a passion for literature and began experimenting with creative writing. His literary debut came in 1929 when his first poem was published in *Green Fields,* the literary supplement of Harbin's *Morning Light Daily*. Subsequently, he wrote the novel The New Grave, which was serialized in the literary supplement of *International Association News*.

From 1929, Kong Luosun served as editor of the literary supplement Bud for the *International Association News*, published weekly. In 1930, after transferring to Changchun for work, he continued editing via correspondence while maintaining his literary output. His poetry: *I Listen Closely* incorporated imagery of factory whistles, indicating that the author's position has become closer to the people and more concerned about the lives of the lower class working people. His short story *Red-Tip Matches* exposed child labor exploitation in match factories. Castration and other works condemned Japanese imperialist brutality in Changchun. These were serialized in Bud. Besides, he published *Disillusion* in *Harbin Five-Day Pictorial* and *Turmoil* in *International Pictorial.*

After the Mukden Incident, *International Association Newspaper* was forcibly shut down. In September 1932, Kong Luosun and his wife departed Harbin for Shanghai.

By 1935, Kong had relocated to Wuhan, where he assumed editorship of *The Violet Thread* , the literary supplement of The *Dagaung Daily*. Beginning in 1937, he collaborated with Feng Naichao and Jiang Xijin to establish *Combat Weekly*, serving as its chief editor. In 1938, he was appointed: council member of the the Chinese Association of Literary and Art Circles for Resisting Enemy based in Hankou and later Chongqing, deputy director of its Publishing Division and editorial board member of the influential journal *Anti Japanese Literature*. By 1940, he had taken on editor-in-chief of *Literary Monthly* in Chongqing and series editor for *Literary Collections*, published by Wenlin Publishing House.

During this period, Kong Luosun maintained prolific, producing: essays: *Wildfire Collection* (1936), *Drizzle* (1942), *The Last Banner* (1943); criticism:

Literary Sketches (1940); story collection: *Loneliness* (1943).

After the founding of the People's Republic of China, Kong Luoshan successively held positions at Nanjing Federation of Literary and Art Circles, Shanghai Writers Association and Shanghai Institute of Literature. In 1978, he was transferred to Beijing to serve as editor-in-chief of *Literary and Art News*, making himself as one of China's most prominent literary critics.

Though not originally from Northeast China, Kong came to the region at age 16 and lived in Harbin and Changchun for an extended period. It was here that he launched his literary career and created works reflecting society in Northeast China at that time. Later went into exile inside Shanhaiguan Pass and continued writing about the anti-Japanese resistance. Among the "Northeastern Writers in Exile" in the 1930s, he undoubtedly deserves a significant place.

Yang Hui（1899—1983）

Yang Hui, originally named Yang Xingdong and also known by his literary name Huixiu, was born in Xiaoyingpan Village, Liaoyang County, Liaoning Province. Like Mu Mutian, Yang Hui was one of the most senior writers among the "Northeastern Writers in Exile." He received his early education in his hometown and enrolled in the Department of Philosophy at Peking University in 1917, where he participated in the patriotic May Fourth Movement. After graduating from Peking University in 1920, he taught at Shenyang First Normal School and later at Taiyuan National Normal College and Ding County (now Dingzhou City), Hebei Province. In 1922, he wrote the socially critical play *Whose Crime*, which exposed the tragedy of a mother-in-law causing the death of her daughter-in-law, earning widespread acclaim. In the summer of 1923, he went to teach at Jimei School in Xiamen and returned to Beijing that autumn, where he published the play *The Guest*. In 1924, he taught at Shandong First Normal School and wrote the poetic drama *Qu Yuan*. In the autumn of 1925, he co-founded the literary group Chenzhong Society in Beijing with Feng Zhi, Chen Weimo, Chen Xianghe, and others. They also launched the literary journal *Chenzhong*, which persisted for nearly nine years and exerted a significant influence on later literary circles. It was hailed as "indeed the most tenacious, sincere, and enduring literary group in China" and "a powerful force in the direction of literature." During this period, Yang Hui taught in Beijing, Tianjin, and other places while continuing his literary creations. He published dramas such as *The Tree of Bitter Tears*, *Celebrating the Full Moon*, *Tears in Laughter*, *New Year's Eve*, and *King Chu Ling*, and also engaged in translating foreign literary works. His drama collection King Chu Ling was published during this time.

During the War of Resistance Against Japanese Aggression, Yang Hui taught in the Chinese Department of Northwest University and at National Central University in Chongqing, where he published literary criticism. In 1947, he moved to Shanghai and taught at the Shanghai Preschool Normal College. In April 1949, he traveled from Hong Kong to Beijing to attend the First National Literary and Arts Congress. He joined the Chinese Communist Party of China in 1950. After the founding of the People's Republic of China, he taught at the Chinese Department of Peking University for many years. He also served as a council member of the Chinese Writers' Association, an academic committee member of Institute of Literature of the Chinese Academy of Social Sciences, and an executive editorial board member of *Literary Review*. His works include the literary critique collection *Literature and Society* and *A Biography of Cao Yu*. His translations include *Prometheus Bound and A Hero of Our Time* and others.

During the War of Resistance Against Japanese Aggression, Yang Hui's achievements were primarily in the creation of wartime dramas. In 1933, he wrote the five-act historical drama *King Chu Ling* which depicts the united resistance of the military and civilians of the Cai State who finally successfully defends their capital, celebrating the inevitable triumph of justice. In contrast, King Chu Ling, who lacked moral virtue and popular support, meets a tragic end, ultimately hanging himself in defeat. This character is rich in satirical significance. Against the backdrop of the escalating nationwide struggle against Japanese aggression, the contemporary relevance of this historical drama was self-evident. Later, Yang Hui attempted to write another historical drama, Wu Zixu, but ultimately left it unfinished.

Yu Heiding（1914—2001）

Yu Heiding's original name was Yu Mindao, and he used the pen name Yu Yan. He was born in Sukou Village, Jimo County, Shandong Province (now Jimo District, Qingdao City).

In his early years, he lived in Northeast China. After the Mukden Incident in 1931, he fled inside Shanhaiguan Pass and began his literary career. In 1933, he joined the Association of Chinese Left-Wing Writers. From 1935 to 1937, his works were published in various Shanghai-based literary magazines such as *Literature*, *Writers*, *Mainstream*, and *Guangming Journal*. Following the August 13th Incident, he left Shanghai and went to Yan'an, where he served as secretary general of the Yan'an Association of Literary and Art Circles for Resisting Enemy, organizing and leading literary and artistic work while writing. In 1945, he moved to the Shansi-Heipei-Shantung-Honan Border Region, serving as executive director and editorial director of the Federation of Literary and Art Circles. Later, he participated in land reform as Deputy Secretary of the Work Committee of the Land Reform Work Corps. In 1948, he arrived in Zhengzhou, where he became deputy director of the Editorial Department of *Central Plains Daily*, the official newspaper of the Central Plains Bureau, and vice chairman of the Central Plains Association of Literary and Art Circles for Resisting Enemy. In 1949, he relocated to Wuhan, holding positions such as director of the Literary and Art Division of the Central-South Bureau's Propaganda Department and director of the Literary and Art Division of the Central South Ministry of Culture. The he served as vice chairman of the Central-South Federation of Literary and Art Circles, chairman and party secretary of the Central-South Writers' Association, chairman of the Wuhan Writers' Association, chairman of the Hubei Federation of Literary and Art Circles, editor-in-chief of *Changjiang Literature & Art*, deputy director of the Wuhan Municipal Propaganda Department, and council member of the Chinese Writers' Association. In 1963, he was transferred to Henan, where he became chairman and party secretary of the Henan Federation of Literary and Art Circles.

Yu Heiding's major works include the short story collection *The Charcoal Kiln*, which depicts the broader lives of soldiers and civilians in liberated areas and Kuomintang-controlled regions during the War of Resistance Against Japanese Aggression. Other works include the novels *Stories of the Countryside* and *Mother and Son*, as well as the critical essays *Writers, Class, and the Era*. After the Mukden Incident, Yu Heiding, along with other Northeastern writers who fled from Northeast China and entered Shanhaiguan Pass, became active in the literary scene inside the Pass, using their writing to reflect the fall of the Northeast. He was regarded as a member of the "Northeastern Writers in Exile." His short story *Shenyang in September* vividly portrays the city's condition after the Mukden Incident, combining realism with sharp critique, and it had a significant impact at the time.

Yu Yifu（1903—1982）

Yu Yifu, originally named Yu Chengze with the courtesy name Yifu, was born in Zhaodong, Heilongjiang Province.

A veteran fighter of the Communist Party of China and an outstanding united front worker, Yu Yifu was also one of the earliest pioneers of New Northeastern Literature. After the Mukden Incident, he primarily engaged in propaganda efforts for the Northeast Salvation Movement and the organizational leadership of cultural work in Northeast China. Due to his limited literary output during this period, many people are less familiar with his contributions.

In 1920, Yu Yifu enrolled in Beijing Advanced Cram School. In 1921, he was admitted to the Mechanical Engineering Department of Tongji University, but due to conflicts with conservative faculty over his reading of progressive literature, he was expelled within six months. By the summer of 1922, he entered Beijing Pingmin University, where he met Professor Xu Dishan, who inspired him to begin writing. In the summer of 1924, he transferred to Yenching University's History Department, marking the start of his literary career. His debut work, *Snow*, was published in the Peking *Morning News Supplement*, vividly depicting the harsh, desolate world of ice and snow in northern China and the oppressive sorrow of impoverished rural life. The piece immediately stood out for its striking realism. Wang Tongzhao, then an editor, praised it in a special note: "Mr. Yu, a native of Heilongjiang and currently studying at Yenching University, possesses an intimate familiarity with life in China's far north, as evidenced in this piece. Regional characteristics from China's unique locales are rarely portrayed in today's literary circles, but recent works like Mr. Gong Tianmin's tragic account and this story have drawn significant attention."

From 1925 to 1927, under his birth name Yu Chengze, Yu Yifu published numerous essays, short stories, and poems in prominent journals such as *Modern Review*, *The Short Story Magazine*, *Yusi*, *Morning News Supplement*, *Peking Press Supplement*, *Yenching University Weekly*, and Shanghai's *Literary Weekly*. During this time, he also became a member of the Chinese

Literature Research Association and served as editorial and business manager for *Yenching University Weekly*.

In 1925, Yu Yifu joined Green Wave Society, a progressive literary group in the New Culture Movement. While in Beijing, he actively contributed to the editing of *Literary Weekly*, taking a clear-cut stand to support Lu Xun and collaborating with figures like Shao Kongliao, Jiao Juyin, Yu Gengyu, Sun Xizhen, and Jiang Gongwei. His works, unflinching in their social critique and humanistic depth, helped propel the first golden decade of modern Chinese literature.

In 1925, Yu Yifu published the short story *The Temple of Cihui* in *Literature Periodical*. The story follows a young man from Northeast China who leaves home in pursuit of career and pure love, only to be crushed by oppressive traditional forces, dying alone in a dilapidated temple far from home. Another story, *He Left in Tears*, explores a similar theme—a disillusioned Northeastern student named Weifu, filled with resentment toward society, departs from home in tears. Yet the author offers no answer: Where can he go? What future awaits him? The protagonist's anguish, hesitation, and despair mirror Yu Yifu's own struggles at the time.

Another recurring theme in Yu's early novel is the suffering of Northeastern farmers amid banditry and war. In *Dawn*, he employs stark, sketch-like prose to depict the brutal murders of Zuping and his elder sister by bandits, the scene punctuated by the hoarse cries of a terrified child. *After Being Buried Alive* tells the horrifying story of Little Haiqing, a boy sentenced to burial alive by militia leader Li Tuanzong simply because his brother was forced into banditry. The boy's final pleas linger like a chilling echo, and the moment "Haiqing's sobs were swallowed by the shuddering earth" is almost unbearable in its suffocating dread. Yet the story ends with a flicker of retribution—Haiqing's brother sneaks back at night to kill Li, offering a grim solace to those still enduring oppression. Yu Yifu's fiction is marked by a tragic grandeur and themes deeply rooted in his era.

Compared to his novels, Yu Yifu's essays and travel writings demonstrate even greater mastery. Works like *Travels Through Jilin and Heilongjiang*, *Notes on a Rural Journey*, *Moonlit Night at Shichahai*, and *Flies* are exceptionally crafted. With effortless grace, he captures everything from the vast, from changing skies of the northern frontier and the lush grasslands of the Songnen Plain to the humblest details—livestock, farmer weddings and funerals, and local folklore. Whether depicting arrogant Japanese invaders or timid farmers, broad fields of soybeans and sorghum, or the rich, earthy scent of the Guandong Plain, his writing is steeped in the distinct essence of the Northeast. The beauty of nature in his works stands in stark contrast to the tragic fates of his characters, creating a profound sense of historical poignancy. On this muddy, troubled land, people struggle forward with unwavering faith, searching for a path toward light. Yu Yifu's writing reflects the transition of Northeast society from darkness to dawn, capturing the dawning awareness of people at a critical historical juncture. For other young Northeastern writers of the time, Yu was not only a literary pioneer but also a seasoned political mentor—truly deserving of the title "elder brother" in both creative and revolutionary endeavors.

After the Mukden Incident, a flood of Northeastern students and youth fled to Peking and Tianjin. By 1936, Yu Yifu served as head of the Propaganda Department of the Northeast Special Work Committee, directly affiliated with the Central Committee's Northern Bureau, where he led propaganda efforts among Northeastern students in exile. He organized the underground publication of the Party, *The Great Wall* and headed the Northeast People's Anti-Japanese Association and the Federation of Northeastern Expatriates in Peking for National Salvation. He also edited salvation journals like *Light of Northeast China*, *Voices of Northeast China*, and *Life in Northeast China*. As a representative of the Party, he extended warm support to progressive Northeastern writers in exile, forging deep friendships with them.

During their exile in Peking, young Northeastern writers such as Jin Zhaoye, Ma Jia, and Shi Guang (author of *Smoke and Dust in Northern Shandong*) received substantial support from Yu Yifu in their anti-Japanese resistance efforts. Yu even helped Li Huiying secure employment, and Li later joined the Northeast National Salvation Association. After the fall of Peking, a large number of students from Peking and Tianjin temporarily gathered in Shandong. At the time, Yu Yifu was in charge of the Jinan Office of the Northeast National Salvation Association, where he arranged for progressive students to travel to the anti-Japanese frontlines. Writers like Ma Jia, Shi Tianshou, and Dong Su and other fellow Northeasterners benefited from his friendship and financial assistance, enabling them to join the national resistance movement.

Following the fall of Shanghai, Yu Yifu relocated to Wuhan in 1938, where he took charge of *Counterattack*, the official publication of the Northeast National Salvation Association. This role brought him into closer contact with many Northeastern writers. He invited Duanmu Hongliang and Xiao Hong to serve as editorial board members of *Counterattack*, while maintaining frequent interactions with Shu Qun, Luo Feng, and Bai Lang, earning deep respect from these Northeastern writers. Under Yu's leadership, over a dozen Northeastern writers contributed to *Counterattack* as either editors or authors.

In 1940, upon learning that Xiao Jun intended to go to the South, Yu Yifu approached Shu Qun three times to discuss the matter, urging that Xiao Jun instead accompany Shu Qun to Yan'an. With meticulous care, Yu arranged for Xiao Jun's family to stay at the headquarters of the Northeast National Salvation Association in Chongqing, then facilitated their safe journey through Baoji and Xi'an, ensuring their arrival in Yan'an without incident.

The following year, under Party directives, Yu Yifu traveled to Hong Kong in his capacity as a leader of the Northeast National Salvation Association. There, he repeatedly assisted Luo Binji and Xiao Hong, addressing their practical difficulties and making them feel the Party's support and warmth. According to Zhou Jingwen's memoirs, when Xiao Hong fell seriously ill, it was Yu Yifu and Duanmu Hongliang who carried her on a stretcher to Zhou's residence. Yu personally inquired about her condition and left detailed instructions for her care before departing. Recognizing the imminent threat of Japanese occupation, Yu assigned a dedicated liaison to oversee Xiao Hong's evacuation from Hong Kong, sternly instructing: "You must not leave Hong Kong until Xiao Hong does. The moment her health permits, she must depart immediately. She is one of our Northeastern writers—a vital cultural asset—and must never fall into Japanese hands!"

After the victory of the War of Resistance Against Japanese Aggression, Yu Yifu served as the chairman of the People's Government of Nenjiang Province. After the founding of the People’s Republic of China, he held a leadership position in Jilin Province. During the ten-year turmoil, Yu Yifu was imprisoned for seven years and suffered physical devastation. He passed away due to illness in 1982.

Yu Yifu paved the way for the emergence of new literature in Northeast China, and contributed greatly to the growth of the "Northeastern Writers in Exile" as a young seedling.

Li Manhong（1917—1942）

Li Manhong's original name was Chen Qingfu, later changed to Chen Mohen, born in Zhuanghe, Liaoning Province. After the Mukden Incident, he fled to the inside Shanhaiguan Pass and studied at the Beijing Zhixing Cram School and the National Northeast Zhongshan Middle School. He actively participated in the December 9th Student Anti Japanese Salvation Movement. During this time, some of his short poems were published in the *Middle School Students* magazine in Peking.

After the full outbreak of the War of Resistance Against Japanese Aggression, Li Manhong drifted as a refugee across Nanjing, Changsha, Guilin, and Chongqing. In 1939, while in Chongqing, he met writers such as Duanmu Hongliang, Xiao Hong, and Zhang Jinyi, balancing his studies with poetry composition. That same year, he enrolled in the Foreign Language Department of Northwest Associated University to study Russian. From 1939 to 1942, under the pen name Li Manhong, he published poems in literary journals such as: *Poetry Creation in Guilin*, *Poetry Reclamation Land in Chongqing*, *Time Literature* in Chongqing. His poetry collection, Red Lantern, was posthumously compiled by his close friend Yao Ben and published as part of the *Modern Literature* Poetry Series, edited by Zhang Jinyi. On June 12, 1942, Li Manhong passed away from illness in Hanzhong, Shaanxi Province, at the young age of 25.

Li Manhong's representative works include his poetry collection Red Lantern and long poem *To My Beloved Homeland.*

Red Lantern comprises thirty-seven poems marked by their widely sourced materials, vibrant forms, unadorned yet fluent language, and intense emotional depth. The collection is unified by a central theme—the struggle for the liberation of the homeland. His poetry blends the profundity of realism with the grandeur of romanticism, creating a distinctive, unrestrained style. Li often employed ordinary objects from daily life to convey profound philosophical insights. In *Matchstick*, he writes: "Though but an inch in length, / A fleeting spark of life— / It ignites the darkness, / Becoming a wildfire that lights the plains." In *Spider*, he declares: "No matter how cunning the insect, / How fearsome the foe— / Should it dare to approach, / Will it not be captured?" *The Spring Thunder* vividly depicts the power of thunder: "The cosmic thunderclap / Shatters the clouds' barricade against the new season... / So mighty its voice! / Striking the solid earth, / It cracks time's frozen grip, / Melting the ice-bound snow." Meanwhile, *Petrel* expresses longing: "Though we rest here tonight in peace, / Our hearts yearn for tomorrow." When read against the backdrop of China's existential crisis during the War of Resistance Against Japanese Aggression and Li's own turbulent exile, these symbolic images—the matchstick lighting the darkness, the thunder melting frozen snow, the petrel yearning for tomorrow, and the spider capturing the invaders—take on profound allegorical meaning. In *Stream*, Li uses flowing water as a metaphor for his revolutionary commitment: "The stream must reach the sea... / And so must the exile!" Here, the stream becomes a call to join the revolutionary tide. Duanmu Hongliang, who knew Li intimately, offered this assessment: "Manhong possessed acute sensitivity and a lucid analytical mind. His emotions were torrential, his inner pitch lofty. Had he been granted more time, he might have developed prominence akin to Mayakovsky's."(From *In Memory of Manhong, Historical Materials of Modern Literature in Northeast China*, Vol. 7)

The thousand-line long poem *To My Beloved Homeland* was written in 1940. Through the autobiographical narrative of "I" in half life experience, the work chronicles the blood-and-fire suffering of the Chinese nation during the 1930s. The poem begins with "my" birth in "the homeland's northeast", expressing the child's deep love for both his native hometown and nation. Later, as "I" drifts into exile - first to Peking where "I" participates in the December 9th Movement, then to Chongqing - the narrator encounters unyielding resistance fighters everywhere and hears salvation's call in every corner. "My" fate becomes inseparable from the motherland's. The poem concludes with this impassioned cry: "O Motherland! For this national revolution's triumph, may Edison's thought and Newton's wisdom flourish! May Marx's genius and Lenin's spirit take root!"

This profoundly autobiographical work reveals the poet's fervent patriotism and unshakable faith in ultimate victory. The poem's majestic momentum, fiery emotion and upward-striving spirit create powerful artistic impact. Li's romantic temperament and sparkling talent burst forth like wind rushing through mountain valleys or unpolished jade awaiting the craftsman's hand - astonishing in its raw brilliance. That such a work, remarkable in both content and form, came from a poet barely 20 years old is truly extraordinary. Because of this, Li Manhong's early death at 25 remains an enduring tragedy of Chinese literature.

Ye Lin（1901—1934）

Ye Lin, originally named Zhang Xingzhi, with the courtesy name He Tiao, also known as Zhang Tiao, used pen names such as Ye Lin, Ye Ling, Ling Yu, E, and L. He was born in Hanting, Weixian County, Shandong Province (now Hanting District, Weifang City).

In 1921, Ye Lin followed his elder brother to Northeast China, living in places like lumber camps in Hulan, where he experienced the lives of the people in the region. In 1922, he left the Northeast China and successively engaged in revolutionary activities and literary creation in Jinan, Qingdao, Hangzhou, and Shanghai. In 1930, he joined the Association of Chinese Left-Wing Writers and was also a top leader and party member of the Shanghai Left-wing Artists Alliance. In 1932, he was dispatched by the Party organization to work in the Central Soviet Zone, where he served as the director of the Ministry of Education of the Fujian-Zhejiang-Jiangxi Soviet Government and concurrently as the principal of Lenin School. Tragically, he passed away in 1934.

Ye Lin was one of the earlier writers to depict the lives of the people in Northeast China. His short story *On the Platform* (published in *Literary Monthly*, Vol. 1, No. 4, 1932) was quite successful. The story draws from Northeastern society in the late 1920s, critiquing the submissive mentality of some farmers while exposing the cruelty of Japanese invaders, offering significant insight. The protagonist is an elderly man living in the forest. To survive, he repeatedly pleads for mercy from the Japanese and his Chinese foreman, only to be mocked and abandoned each time. Eventually, he is caught as a thief by the Japanese on the platform of Changchun Station, where he is tormented, humiliated, and degraded. He becomes a docile slave, a pitiable creature desperate to please his Japanese masters—flapping his ears and mimicking Japanese phrases like "Ariyato" to amuse Japanese officers and prostitutes. In *Miscellaneous Notes During the Cloudy Period*, Hu Feng provided a detailed analysis of this story:

One moment he lies on the ground, the next he sits up; he imitates a camel, then a Buddha—his tricks never end. The Japanese order him to eat dirty snow from the ground, so he kneels and licks it up like a cat. Then they command him to bark like a dog, so he tilts his head, flaps his ears, and barks, even mimicking a hoarse-voiced dog...

What kind of scene is this? Even before the final moment—when a green club cuts through the air with a hiss before crashing onto his skull—the reader is already left unbearably shaken.

Hu Feng noted that the author's approach "exudes a sense of realism" and demonstrates "a proactive spirit" in handling the subject matter. Though the story portrays the numb, trampled soul of a Northeastern farmer, it carries a deeper, thought-provoking significance. As Hu Feng remarked: "This work has not lost its vitality even now. Reading it, we can still feel the author's unyielding spirit burning in the text."

As a pioneer of progressive literature in Northeast China, Ye Lin and his story *On the Platform* remain worthy of remembrance.

Yang Shuo（1913—1968）

Yang Shuo, originally named Yang Yujin, also used the pen names Yang Baoshu and Ying Shu. He was born in Penglai, Shandong Province.

Yang Shuo was a renowned modern Chinese writer and a master of prose. In his youth, he lived in Harbin, where he began his literary career. In 1937, he left Northeast China and moved inside Shanhaiguan Pass. In 1939, he joined Writer's Battlefield Visiting Group to North China, accompanying the Eighth Route Army for wartime reporting. By 1942, he had arrived in Yan'an. He continued to work with the military and later participated in the War to Resist US Aggression and Aid Korea. After 1954, he devoted himself to professional writing and international cultural exchange. His prose is celebrated for its fresh, lively style and precise language, establishing a unique and influential literary voice. Yang Shuo was persecuted to death during the Cultural Revolution.

During the War of Resistance Against Japanese Aggression, Yang Shuo was regarded as one of the "Northeastern Writers in Exile". This classification stems from his early 1930s residency in Harbin, where he lived for an extended period and engaged in literary creation before exiling from the Northeast inside Shanhaiguan Pass—a trajectory shared by many other Northeastern writers.

Before 1936, Yang Shuo worked as a bank clerk in Daoli District, Harbin. During this time, he published several poems, predominantly in classical forms, in Harbin's *International Association News*, *Harbin Five-Day Pictorial*, and the "Night Watch" supplement of Changchun's *Datong Daily*. Notable works include: *Seeking Spring in Majiagou*, *Lament for Spring*, *Song of Falling Leaves and Cicadas*, *Withered Spring Heart*, *This Morning*. He also wrote the theme *Snowflakes Drifting Over Manchuria*, which depicts an anti-Japanese youth's rebellion against society and subsequent escape from the Northeast. The narrative, poignant and deeply personal, reflects Yang Shuo's own emotional struggles. Overall, Yang Shuo's works from this period were not yet fully mature, and his output was relatively limited. Nevertheless, his experiences and writings solidify his place among the "Northeastern Writers in Exile".

Chen Xinlao (dates of birth and death unknown)

Information about Chen Xinlao is relatively scarce. As one of the younger members of the "Northeastern Writers in Exile", he was of similar age to Gao Tao and Li Manhong. A diligent and highly talented poet, his life was tragically cut short. In the 11th issue of Changchun in 1980, Li Huiying published an article titled*3* which includes valuable historical accounts of Xinlao. An excerpt follows:

Chen Xinlao, a poet originally from Heilongjiang, fled to Shanghai after the Mukden Incident, living a life of uncertainty where one meal was never guaranteed to follow another... People called him 'Chen.' Pale and frail, his poor health made him afflicted with tuberculosis tuberculosis. He passed away in 1945. Chen was a true Northeastern poet, yet he has often been overlooked. Poetry was an unprofitable craft—selling a poem couldn't even buy two bowls of plain noodles. What a world we live in. I wrote a few more lines for him here as a small act of remembrance.

Jiang Chunfang (1912-1988)

Jiang Chunfang was born in 1912 into a shop clerk's family in Changzhou, Jiangsu Province. After graduating from elementary school in 1928, he moved with his family to Harbin. In 1931, he joined the Anti-Imperialist League, and in 1932, he became a full member of the Communist Party of China. As a propaganda officer for the Manchurian Provincial Committee of the CPC, he actively promoted progressive cultural activities in Harbin alongside Luo Feng, Shu Qun, and Jin Jianxiao. He also edited the underground party publication *Manchurian Red Flag*, and his home served as a secret party headquarters. In 1936, he was arrested for his involvement in founding the Great Northern Pictorial but was later rescued from prison.

During this period, Jiang Chunfang published numerous works—primarily critical essays—in *International Association Newspaper* and *Greater North New Daily*. His notable writings include: *From "New Year" to "Old Age"*, *The Plight of German Literature*, *Return to the Spring of My Homeland*, *The Great Road*, *Literary Heritage*, *Content and Technique* , *Literature as a Tool*, *Futurism*, *Exploring Spring*, *The Futility of Literature*, *Mass Art and Vulgar Tastes*, *The Fourth Type of Person* and *High-Heeled Shoes*.

In 1938, Jiang Chunfang moved to Shanghai, where he worked at Asia Film Company, promoting and distributing Soviet films. During this period, he initiated the establishment of the Sino-Soviet Film Workers Association. By 1941, he became the editor-in-chief of *Time Weekly*, and in 1945, he assumed leadership roles as editor-in-chief of *Time Daily* and president of Time Publishing House.

After the founding of the People's Republic of China, he served as the director of the Drama Department of the Shanghai Military Control Commission, the director of the External Cultural Liaison Office of the Municipal Cultural Bureau, and the principal of the Shanghai Russian School. In 1952, he was transferred to the position of director of the Stalin Works Translation Office of the Central Propaganda Department, and in 1953, he became the deputy director of the Marx, Engels, Lenin and Stalin Works Compilation Bureau. He was persecuted and imprisoned during the Cultural Revolution. In 1975, he was released from prison and served as the deputy director of the editorial board of the *Encyclopedia of China* and the editor in chief of the Encyclopedia Publishing House.

Jiang Chunfang dedicated his life to cultural leadership and was one of the pioneering figures in advancing progressive culture in Northeast China.

Shi Tianshou（1911—1995）

Shi Tianshou (original name: Tian Zhicheng) was born in Fuyu, Jilin Province.

From 1920 to 1931, he attended elementary and secondary school in Fuyu County and Jilin City, where he gradually developed an interest in literature and art. After the Mukden Incident, he fled to Peking and studied at Hongda Academy while beginning to publish works in the literary supplement *Fire Plow* of Jilin's *Republican News*. In 1933, he joined the Association of Chinese Left-Wing Writers, and in 1934, he enrolled at Peking University, concurrently serving as a group leader of the Peking Association of Chinese Left-Wing Writers. In 1936, he joined the Chinese National Liberation Vanguard Corps and later moved to Nanjing, Shanxi, and Wuhan, working as a Minxian cadre. By October 1938, he arrived in Yan'an.

During his time in Yan'an, Shi Tianshou held several important positions including party branch secretary and secretary of the Organization Department of the Border Region of the Chinese Association of Literary and Art Circles for Resisting Enemy, and secretary of the Cultural Work Team of the 718th Regiment in the 359th Brigade. He published essays such as *Yan'an* in *Jiefang Daily* and the short story Madness in 1939, which celebrated the patriotic anti-imperialist spirit of a truck driver. His short story collection *Burning* was published in 1949. While serving as secretary of the work team in the 718th Regiment of the 359th Brigade, he wrote numerous works reflecting the lives of soldiers and civilians in Nanniwan, which were published in *Jiefang Daily*.

After the victory of the War of Resistance Against Japanese Aggression, Shi Tianshou was dispatched to Northeast China with a cadre team. He successively held the following positions: reporter for *Northeast Daily*, secretary-director and team leader of the Grain Reserve Work Team under the Civil Affairs Department of Jilin Provincial People's Government, team leader of the South Jilin Administrative Office Work Team, county magistrate of Shuangyang County, Jilin Province. Following the founding of the People's Republic of China, he served in several important roles: director of Jilin Provincial Department of Education, deputy director of Jilin Provincial Culture and Education Committee, vice chairman of Northeast Writers Association, executive vice chairman and deputy party secretary of Shenyang Writers Association. His major literary works include: fiction and reportage collection *At the Forefront* (1955), narrative poem *The Story of Grandpa and Grandma* (1956), depicting anti-Japanese struggles, narrative poem *Singing of Nanniwan* (1957), extolling the Nanniwan spirit, poetry collection *Song of the Screw*, literary criticism collection *Red Rain Collection*, medium length novel *Sisters-in-Law's Rivalry* and *The Mainstay*, novel *Reclaiming Nanniwan*, and *Selected Short Stories of Shi Tianshou*. Shi Tianshou enjoyed a long and prolific writing career, producing works that covered diverse themes with rich content and strong contemporary relevance. After 1949, he spent extended periods living in Dalian to immerse himself in local life.

Cai Tianxin（1915—1983）

Cai Tianxin (original name: Cai Guozheng, Cai Jie; pen names: Cai Zhe, Jun Mo, Bai Shi, etc.) was born in Changjiawanzi Village, Shenyang City, Liaoning Province.

In 1933, while studying at Shenyang's Wen Hui High School, he began his literary career with the debut essay *Homecoming*. In 1934, his short story *Starvation* was published in Dalian's *Taidong Daily*. After graduating high school in 1935, he enrolled in the Chinese Department of Shandong University, where he founded the New Literature Society and edited the literary supplement *New Ground* for *Qingdao People's Daily*. He joined the Chinese National Liberation Vanguard Corps in 1936. In 1937, his medium length novel *Valley of the Northeast* was published in Shanghai's *Literary Grove*.

During the War of Resistance Against Japanese Aggression, he studied at Sichuan University as a visiting student, editing: *Fortnightly Literature* and *Iron Stream*, literary supplement of *Xinmin Bao*. He joined the Communist Party of China in 1938. By 1940, he reached Yan'an, serving as: secretary & researcher at the Literature Theory Research Office of Central Research Institute, participant in the 1942 Yan'an Forum on Literature and Art. There, he wrote the medium length novel *Mountain Village Father and Daughter*.

In 1945, he returned to Northeast China and successively held the following positions: director of the Propaganda Section, Liaoxi Province, deputy director of the Propaganda Department, First Prefectural Committee of Liaoxi (during which he assisted in publishing the journal *The Grassland*). Later he served as: professor at Jilin University, president of Liaoning College. After the founding of the People's Republic of China, he assumed the following positions: director of the Editing and Publishing Department, Northeast Federation of Literary and Art Circles, editor-in-chief of *Northeast Literature*, secretary-general of Northeast Federation of Literary and Art Circles, vice chairman & deputy party secretary of Shenyang Branch of Chinese Writers Association.

Cai Tianxin's other major literary works include: short story collection *Under the Changbai Mountains*, depicting anti-Japanese resistance in Northeast China, *Early Spring Days*, *By the Weiqing River*, *Support*, *Restlessness*, depicting life of agricultural cooperation, novels: *The Youth of the Land*, *Storm Over the Hun River* and essays, literary criticism, and poetry.

Liu Shude（1906—1970）

Liu Shu De, pen names: Di Xian, Nangong Dongguo, etc., was born in Xinlitun Village, Yongji County, Jilin Province.

Following the Mukden Incident, Liu Shude fled to Peking, where he pursued self-education at the National Library of China. Later, he enrolled in the Chinese Department of China University and began his literary career. In 1935, his short story *Journey Through the Northern Frontier* was published in Peking's *Middle School Student*. After the fall of Peking, he wandered southward to Yunnan, teaching at secondary schools while longing for his homeland in the Northeast. During this period, he wrote works such as *Autumn Affairs and Spring Mud* , *The Melon Peddler*. When the Japanese invaded Yunnan, his novels took on a more somber tone, expressing his anguish over the war and society through stories like *Lost* , *Torment*, *Shadow of the Pagoda*.

From 1948 to 1952, Liu Shude returned to Changchun and taught at Changchun University before going back to teach at Kunming Normal University. In 1952, he was transferred to work at the Yunnan Federation of Literary and Art Circles. After 1955, he assumed several important positions: vice chairman of the Kunming Branch of Chinese Writers Association, council member of the Chinese Writers Association, deputy director of the Research Institute under the Yunnan Branch of Chinese Academy of Sciences. Liu Shude was persecuted to death during the Cultural Revolution. In 1978, Yunnan People's Publishing House published *Selected Novels of Liu Shude*.

After fleeing inside Shanhaiguan Pass, Liu Shude resided in Yunnan for an extended period, developing a distinctive literary style that blended northern and southern regional characteristics with strong individuality. His works includes: short stories: *The Bridge*, *Old Toughie*; novel: *Homecoming*; short story collection: *Selling the Plow*, all of which received high praise.

Qiu Qin（1915-2006）

Qiu Qin, originally named Deng Tianyou, was born in Bin County, Heilongjiang Province.

Following the Mukden Incident, he fled inside Shanhaiguan Pass. In 1934, he studied at Northeastern University in Peking. After the outbreak of the December 9th Student Movement in 1935, he joined the Student News Agency led by the Peking Student Union and the Peking Literary Youth Association, where he served as editor for the literary supplement *Literary Youth* in *Oriental Express*. In 1936, he published his poem Grief in Peking's *Poetry Magazine*, followed by his well-received work *Qin River Grass*.

During the War of Resistance Against Japanese Aggression, Qiu Qin participated in resistance efforts across northern Shandong, Xuzhou, southeastern Shanxi, and Chongqing. He served as deputy head of the field service corps in the Northeast Army's 51st Corps, joined the Northeast National Salvation Association as an editorial committee member for its journal *Counterattack*, and later served on the editorial board of *Literary Monthly* in Chongqing. His poem *Gelang Wall*, published in Chongqing's *Ta Kung Pao*, gained considerable popularity.

After the founding of the People's Republic of China, Qiu Qin worked as a secretary at the Sino-Soviet Friendship Association in Beijing and joined the Chinese Writers' Association in 1955. In 1966, he was transferred to serve as deputy head of the Asia-Africa-Latin America Cultural Research Institute under the Commission for Cultural Relations with Foreign Countries, and later worked at the Institute for the History of Natural Sciences, Chinese Academy of Sciences.

Not only was Qiu Qin an accomplished poet, but he also distinguished himself as an outstanding translator of Soviet literature. His major translations include: *Selected Soviet Poems*, *The Poetry of Nazim Hikmet*, *The Poetry of Tikhonov*, *Selected Poems and Prose of Ivan Franko*, *Selected Works of Mayakovsky*, *The Poetry of Tokombaev*, and *Terkin in the Other World*.

Liu Zhiming（1905-1968）

Liu Zhiming, originally named Chen Zujian, was born in Gaiping, Liaoning Province (now Gaizhou City, Yingkou).

He was an outstanding organizer of literary and artistic work in Northeast China.

In his youth, Liu Zhiming studied in Japan, where he was exposed to Marxism-Leninism. He graduated from Waseda University in Japan in 1929. After returning to China the same year, he joined revolutionary work in Shanghai and became a member of the Communist Party of China in 1931. He served as the president of the Northeast National Salvation Association, a council member of the Shanghai Anti-Japanese National Salvation Federation, and the Party group secretary of the China's Territorial Security Alliance. In 1933, he was arrested and imprisoned but was released in 1937. During the War of Resistance Against Japanese Aggression, after arriving in Yan'an, he held positions such as director of the Academic Affairs Office of the Central Party School, head of the Third Department of the Party School, and president of the Yan'an Peking Opera Theater.

In 1942, Liu Zhiming organized and led comrades from the Party School Club to create and perform the acclaimed Peking opera *Forced to the Liangshan*, which was highly praised by all sectors in Yan'an. Later, he collaborated with comrades from the Yan'an Peking Opera Research Institute to produce another excellent Peking opera *Three Attacks on Zhu Village*, which also received widespread acclaim.

After the victory of the War of Resistance Against Japanese Aggression, Liu Zhiming went to Northeast China, where he successively served as secretary and mayor of the Anshan Municipal Committee, deputy secretary of the Andong (now Dandong) Prefectural Party Committee, deputy head of the Propaganda Department of the Liaodong Sub-bureau of the CPC Central

Committee, deputy head of the Propaganda Department of the Northeast Bureau of the CPC Central Committee, minister of the Culture Ministry of the Northeast People's Government, and chairman of the Northeast Association of Literary and Art Circles for Resisting Enemy. At the First National Literature and Arts Congress in 1949, he served as the head of the Northeast delegation. During his time in Northeast China, Liu Zhiming extensively united literary and artistic local workers from all fields, promoting the flourishing development of literature and art in the Northeast liberated areas and the early years of the People's Republic of China. He presided over and participated in the creation of outstanding Peking operas such as *Yandang Mountains* and *The Beauty Trap*, the Pingju opera *The Son-in-Law*, and the drama *In the Face of New Things*.

After 1953, Liu Zhiming served successively as Vice Minister of the Ministry of Culture, Vice Chairman and Secretary-General of the National Federation of Literary and Art Circles, and Executive Council Member of the Chinese Dramatists Association. He published numerous commentaries and speeches on the development and reform of Chinese theater. Unfortunately, he was persecuted to death during the Cultural Revolution.

Jin Zhaoye（1912—1995）

Jin Zhaoye, originally named Jin Yutong, was born in Liaozhong County, Liaoning Province (now Liaozhong District, Shenyang Province). He was of Manchu ethnicity, belonging to the Aisin Gioro clan.

After the Mukden Incident in 1931, he fled to Peking and Tianjin, where he enrolled in Lianhua Film Company to study art. However, in 1932, he abandoned his artistic pursuits to join the Anti-Japanese Volunteer Army, engaging in resistance activities in western Liaoning and northern Hebei. After half a year, when the Volunteer Army collapsed, Jin Zhaoye returned to Peking and resumed his life as a refugee.

In 1933, Jin joined the Peking Woodcut Research Society, where he studied woodcut art while also beginning his literary career. His works were published in newspapers such as *Peking Press*, *Beichen Daily*, *Ta Kung Pao*, *Yong Pao*, *Northern Daily*, and *North China Daily*. He also participated in the Anti-Imperialist League and, in 1934, joined the Association of Chinese Left-Wing Writers. During this time, he began corresponding with Lu Xun on the subject of woodcut art.

In 1938, Jin Zhaoye went to Yan'an. After the founding of the People's Republic of China, he worked in the Liaoning Provincial Government, holding positions such as director of the Department of Agriculture and deputy director of the Planning Commission. In 1965, he was transferred to the International Liaison Department of the CPC Central Committee.

Dong Su（1918—1994）

Dong Su, originally named Dong Xueheng, was born in Yushu, Jilin Province.

In 1934, Dong Su fled from Jilin to Peking and studied at Northeast Zhongshan High School, where she participated in the December 9th Movement. In 1936, she was admitted to Peking University's Women's College of Liberal Arts. After the July 7th Incident in 1937, she joined the Anti-Japanese National Salvation Movement and became a member of the Communist Party of China in Wuhan in 1938. She then worked in propaganda for the Fourth Detachment of the New Fourth Army. Later, she went to Yan'an, where she served as an instructor at the Anti-Japanese Military and Political University and the Women's University, and worked at the United Front Work Department of the CPC Central Committee and the Literature and Art

Research Office of the Central Research Institute. In 1942, she was transferred as a war correspondent for the 359th Brigade of the Eighth Route Army.

In 1941, Dong published her first short story, *The Blood Seller*, followed by a series of reportage works in Yan'an.

After the victory of the War of Resistance Against Japanese Aggression, Dong Su returned to Northeast China, where she successively served as head of the Propaganda Department of the Shuangyang County Committee and deputy director of the Propaganda Department of the Jilin Provincial Committee. During the Cultural Revolution, she was arranged to settle in rural areas for two years. After the downfall of the Gang of Four, she was reappointed as the minister of Propaganda of the Jilin Provincial Party Committee, and in 1983, she was appointed as the deputy director of the Standing Committee of the Jilin Provincial People's Congress.

Dong Su's literary works also include the short stories *Zhang Yulan*, *Misunderstanding*, and *One Heart Within and Without*, published in *Northeast Literature and Art* after the founding of the People's Republic of China. In 1951, her short story collection *Granny Sun's New Days* was published by Northeast People's Publishing House. In 1963, she contributed the revolutionary story *In the Cradle of Revolution* to the journal *Changchun*. Additionally, she published theoretical essays on literature and art in publications such as *Fenjin*, *Film Literature*, *Changchun*, and *Jilin Literature*. After 1983, she wrote over a dozen short stories, including *Turning into Spring Mud to Nurture Flowers* and *She Advances Through Hardship*, as well as three medium length novels such as *Figures in Turbulent Times*, along with more than twenty essays, totaling nearly 300,000 words.

Dong Su was a member of the Chinese Writers Association, a committee member of the China Federation of Literary and Art Circles, and served as Chairman of the Jilin Provincial Federation of Literary and Art Circles and Honorary Chairman of the Jilin Writers Association.

Lei Jia (1915–2009)

Lei Jia, originally named Liu Tianda, was born in Dandong, Liaoning Province.

In 1929, he attended middle school in Shenyang. After the Mukden Incident, he fled inside Shanhaiguan Pass and, along with many patriotic youths, petitioned in Nanjing to reclaim lost territory. In 1935, he studied in Japan, where he came into contact with progressive student groups such as the Chinese Dramatists Association. Returning to China in 1937, he published literary theory articles in *Literary Guide* and *World Trends*, edited by Bai Xiaoguang (Ma Jia), as well as essays and feature stories in *Ta Kung Pao* and *Battlefield*.

In 1938, Lei Jia went to Yan'an, where he studied at the Chinese People's Anti-Japanese Military and Political University and joined the Communist Party of China. Later, he worked in propaganda in the Central Hebei Anti-Japanese Base Area. In 1939, he returned to Yan'an and engaged in professional writing under the Yan'an Association of Literary and Art Circles for Resisting Enemy. He published short stories such as *A Type 38 Rifle*, *Yalu River*, *Yellow River Evening Song*, and *The Road* in *Literary Front*, *Front of Literature and Art*, *Jiefang Daily*, and *Military-Political Journal of the Eighth Route Army*, depicting the lives of frontline soldiers. Among these, *A Type 38 Rifle* gained significant acclaim.

After 1942, Lei Jia immersed himself in rural life, serving as a local cadre for three years, and wrote two short story collections, *Water Tower* and *Male and Female Heroes*, which portrayed life in the liberated rural areas.

After the victory of the War of Resistance Against Japanese Aggression, Lei Jia returned to Northeast China and served as the director of the Dandong Paper Mill. In 1951, he was transferred to Beijing, where he engaged in professional writing at the Central Literary Research Institute and the Chinese

Writers' Association, later becoming the vice chairman of the Beijing Writers' Association. As a prolific writer, he produced a substantial body of work. His major works include the novel *My Holiday*, the *Potential* trilogy—*Spring Comes to the Yalu River*, *Standing in the Forefront*, and *The Blue Maple Woods*—as well as essay collections such as *May Flowers*, *Notes from Visits to Hungary and Czechoslovakia*, and *From Ice Peaks to Great Rivers*, and the short story collection *The Call of Youth*. After the downfall of the Gang of Four, he wrote feature stories and short novels, including *May Rain*, *White Silk Flowers*, *She Is Among Us*, and *The Roaring Yellow River*.

Other "Northeastern Writers in Exile"

Ye Youquan A native of Shenyang, Ye Youquan was originally a student at Northeastern University, studying in the College of Liberal Arts. He maintained frequent contact with classmates in Northeastern University such as Bai Xiaoguang (Ma Jia), Zhang Luwei, Zhao Xianwen, Shen Changyan, and Lin Jirong. Ye often wrote literary theory articles. After the Mukden Incident, he went into exile in Peking, where he co-edited *Literary Guide* with Bai Xiaoguang and opposed Zhang Luwei, who later became a traitorous collaborator. During the War of Resistance Against Japanese Aggression, he engaged in resistance and national salvation work. He also worked at the Jilin Academy of Social Sciences.

Li Manlin A young exiled poet and literary figure in Peking, Li Manlin published the influential poetry collection *Sorghum Leaves* in 1935. He passed away tragically before the July 7th Incident.

Gao Tao An exiled Northeastern student in Peking and a member of the Peking Association of Chinese Left-Wing Writers, Gao Tao, whose pen name is Qi Tong, gained acclaim for his novel *The New Generation*, which depicted the December 9th Student Movement. He was also a translator, known for translating Fyodor Dostoevsky's *The Insulted and the Injured* into Chinese.

Tian Feng An exiled Northeastern student in Peking and an underground CPC member, Tian Feng was also part of the Peking Association of Chinese Left-Wing Writers. He published novels and essays in Shanghai's *Mainstream*. After the fall of Peking, he fled to Taiyuan in 1937, where he perished in a Japanese air raid.

Li Wei Originally named Li Bingchen, Li Wei fled to Peking after the Mukden Incident and studied at Tsinghua University. He edited *New Ground*, a publication of the Association of Chinese Left-Wing Writers, and also translated Soviet literary works.

Shi Guang A former philosophy student at Northeastern University, Shi Guang went into exile in Peking after the Mukden Incident. While pursuing his own writing, he edited Oriental Express. After the fall of Peking, he worked on the journal *Counterattack* in Wuhan. His published works include the novel *Smoke and Dust in Northern Shandong*. During the War of Resistance Against Japanese Aggression, he joined the Yan'an Association of Literary and Art Circles for Resisting Enemy. After the founding of the People's Republic of China, he worked in Liaoning and served as vice president of the Liaoning Academy of Social Sciences before retirement.

Li Lei A student at Northeastern University, Li Lei went into exile in Peking where he gained recognition for his poetry, among which *Wanderer's Song* is relatively notable. After the outbreak of the War of Resistance Against Japanese Aggression, he moved to Yan'an and engaged in literary creation at the Association of Literary and Art Circles.

Guo Weicheng A high school student in Shenyang before the Mukden Incident, Guo Weicheng founded the progressive literary publication *Ice Flower* with his classmates and received support from the Communist Party of Manchuria Provincial Committee. Comrade Liu Shaoqi, who was working in the Provincial Committee at the time, sent someone to contact them. Guo

Weicheng fled to Peking after the Mukden Incident and wrote poetry and prose. Later, he participated in the revolution and served as the minister of Railways after the founding of the People's Republic of China.

Di Geng A poet from Hunchun, Jilin Province, Di Geng wrote the poem *Between the White Mountains and Black Waters* during his exile in Peking. Serialized in Shanghai in 1937, it was met with widespread acclaim.

Ji Feng Originally named Li Fuyu, Ji Feng was a student at Northeastern University and an underground CPC member. After fleeing to Peking, he published fiction in magazines such as *Literary Guide*.

Liu Heijia Originally named Liu Zhihong, Liu Heijia began writing in 1940. He was forced into exile in Fujian, Chongqing, Chengdu, Guilin, and other regions, and published his works. After the founding of the People's Republic of China, he worked for many years in Shenyang.

Chen Wei Originally named Chen Lijuan, Chen Wei was born in Shanghai in 1917. In 1933, she moved to Harbin, where she befriended progressive writers such as Jiang Chunfang, Xiao Jun, and Xiao Hong, and actively participated in the Harbin Harmonica Society, a progressive literary group. Under the pen name "Xiaomao", she published literary works like *The Little Old Woman*, *The Girl and the Gentleman*, *See If You Can Laugh*, and *Xiao Mao and Her Father* in *Greater North New Daily* and *International Cooperation Daily*. Returning to Shanghai at the end of 1936, she engaged in progressive literary activities, attended the Sino-French Drama School, and published *A Letter to a Certain Writer* in Shanghai's *Qianqiu* in 1944. In 1947, she worked as an editor at *Time Daily* and continued publishing. After 1949, she was employed at the Shanghai Film Studio, translating foreign films.

Luo Muhua Before the Mukden Incident, Luo Muhua taught at Wenhui Middle School in Xinmin County, Liaoning Province (now Xinmin City). An early poet in the Northeast New Literature Movement, he published works in Shanghai's *Poetry Journal* and Peking's *Morning Post*.

Appendix: List of Writers During the Northeast Occupation Period

(Due to limited historical records, omissions and inaccuracies may exist. This list is for reference only.)

Jin Jianxiao (pen names Jianxiao, Balai, Jian, JK, Liu Qian, Jian Shuo)

Tian Ben (also known as Hua Xilu, pen name Shanchuan Caocao)

Guan Monan (pen names Monan, Dongyan, Bogai, Meng Lai, Mo Nan, Shi Kangdi)

Chen Di (formerly known as Liu Guoxing, pen names Man Di, Shu Ying, Ba Li, Yi Ni, Liu Wei, Jiang Xingmin, Yu Quming, Guo Xing, Jiang Qiao, He Wei, Du Ming)

Deng Li (formerly known as Liang Menggeng, pen names Shan Ding, Liang Shan Ding, Jing Ren, Xiao Qian, Liang Mou, Mao Ye, A Geng)

Fang Weiai (pen names Lin Lang, Fang Xi, Fang Xi)

Li Keyi (pen name Yuan Xi, real name Hao Qingsong)

Wu Baixin (formerly known as Wu Yuhong)

Ma Xun (pen name Jin Yin, Xiang Di, S · D)

Sima Sangdun (pen names Wang Guangti and Jin Ming)

Xin Feng (formerly known as Zhang Boyan)

Luo Mingzhe (pen names Luo Qi, Luo Yongqian, Di Fan, Zhang Che, Luo Bei)

Guo Yao (formerly known as Gao Desheng and Gao Yeping, pen names Sa Hua, Sa Hua, Guo Dongyao, Yan Chizhu, Zhuang Moru, Wu Chuan, Shi Zhe, Ye Deng, Wu Ai, Qi Hong, Wu Lang, Ji Zhe)

Liu Danhua (formerly known as Liu Changqing, pen names Sen, Sen Cong, Yi Jianshuang, Xia Dan, Dan Yu, Ou Yu)

Li Qiao (formerly known as Li Gongyue, pen name Ye He)

Cheng Xian (formerly known as Cheng Jun, pen names Xue Zhu, Cheng Xue Zhu, Cheng Xuan, Nai He Tang, Qing Dao Ren)

Tian Lin (pen names Dan Di, Xiao Xi, Tian Xiang, An Di)

Mei Niang (formerly known as Sun Jiarui)

Zuo Di (formerly known as Luo Mai, pen names Zhi, Jin Tan, He Qi, Ba Er, Zuo Yi, Luo Mai)

Ye Li (formerly known as Liu Fangqing, pen names Ye Li, Jing Hai, Liu Ming)

Tian Bing (formerly known as Li Beikai, Li Hejia, pen names Man Liqi, Li Ye, Ai Xiang)

Wang Qiuying (formerly known as Wang Zhiping, pen names Qiu Ying, Su Ke, Shu Ke)

Yu Qiwen (also known as Yu Qingfei, pen names Tie Han and Zhi Shalang)

Lu Qi (formerly known as Lu Qizhi, pen names Hua Qing, Hua Yuan, Feng Yuan, Xiao Ni)

Bai Tuofang (formerly known as Yu Mingren, pen names Nu Li, Yu Yiqiu, Tian Lang, Bai Hua)

Bai Shi (formerly known as Bai Zhengguang, pen names Wei Ling, Ying Di)

Zhang Qingyu (pen name Bai Ling, Qing Yu)

Zhang Qingji (pen names Yi Yun, Mu Ren, Mu Yin)

Jin Tang (formerly known as Jin Debin, pen names Hei Mengbai, Jin Shan, Tian Yue, Fei Ying, Yi Shui)

Gao Baicang (pen names Cui Bochang, Cui Shu, Yu Youyu)

Meng Su (also known as Wang Mengsu, pen name Gu Ying)

Li Zhengzhong (pen names Ke Ju and Wei Changming)

Zhao Mengyuan (pen names Xiaosong, Mengyuan, Bai Yeyue, MY)

Yi Chi (pen names Yi Chi and Liu Yuzhang)

Hong Yuan (formerly known as Ma Huan, pen name Li Xingjian)

Ling Fei (pen name Wei Ming)

Sui Die (pen name Tong Zisong)

An Xi (also known as An Fenglin)

Shi Zu (pen name Chen Yin)

Bian Hezhi

Shi Jun

Wai Wen

Wu Ying

Mu Rugai (originally named Mu Duli, later renamed Mu Duli, Mu Chenggong, Mu Liutian, born in 1885, Beijing, Manchu)

Wu Lang (formerly known as Ji Shouren)

Huang Manqiu

Du Baiyu

Wen Guang

Liu Mo

Leng Ge

Wang Ze

Lei Daopu

Ai Ren

Yang Cideng

Gu Yi

Xin Shi

Xin Jia

Shi Ming

Yi He

Li Jifeng (formerly known as Li Fuyu, pen names Li Jifeng, Ji Feng, Lei Leisheng, Yi Zui, Fang Jin, born in 1917, from Liaoyang)

Chen Ying (formerly known as Chen Haohui)

Ke Ju (formerly known as Li Zhengzhong, pen name Li Mo)

www.ingramcontent.com/pod-product-compliance
Lightning Source LLC
LaVergne TN
LVHW010650110826
845149LV00014B/3020